D1575186

Friends of the Heart

Emilie Barnes
& Donna Otto

HARVEST HOUSE PUBLISHERS
Eugene, Oregon 97402

Except where otherwise indicated, all Scripture quotations in this book are taken from the New King James Version NKJV, Copyright © 1979, 1980, 1982 by Thomas Nelson, Inc., Publishers. Used by permission.

Cover by Left Coast Design, Portland, Oregon

Photographs are copyrighted by Kendra Dew Photographic, Inc., Berkley, Michigan, and may not be reproduced without permission from the photographer.

FRIENDS OF THE HEART
Copyright © 1999 by Harvest House Publishers
Eugene, Oregon 97402

Library of Congress Cataloging-in-Publication Data

Barnes, Emilie.
  Friends of the heart / Emilie Barnes, and Donna Otto: with
Anne Christian Buchanan.
        p.   cm.
  ISBN 1-56507-990-6
    1. Christian women—Religious life.   2. Female friendship—Religious
aspects—Christianity.   I. Otto, Donna.   II. Buchanan, Anne Christian.
III. Title.
BV4527.B3587   1999
241'.6762'082—dc21   99-21979
                                                                          CIP

All rights reserved. No portion of this book may be reproduced in any form without the written permission of the Publisher.

Printed in the United States of America.

99 00 01 02 03 04 / DH / 10 9 8 7 6 5 4 3 2 1

For Donna's friends
and for Emilie's friends,
and for the friends we share
and for the friends who
told us your stories . . .
You all have an honored place
in the gallery of our hearts.

L♥ L♥ L♥

Contents

L♥ L♥ L♥

Prologue

The Gallery of Our Hearts

Kindred spirits are not so scarce as I used to think. It's splendid to find out there are so many of them in the world.

—LUCY MAUD MONTGOMERY,
Anne of Green Gables

♪ ♪ ♪

If you're like most women we know, you have at least one photo gallery somewhere in your home.

If you're like us, your entire *home* is practically a photo gallery.

That's one thing the two of us—Donna and Emilie—have learned we have in common as friends. Our walls, our tabletops, even our refrigerator doors (or, in Donna's case, the freezer door in the pantry) are crowded with the faces of people we love: Our husbands, David and Bob, in a number of dapper poses. Our children and Emilie's precious grandchildren at a variety of ages—from baby bonnets to snaggletooth grins to prom dresses to wedding-wear and beyond. Parents and in-laws, too, plus an assortment of sepia-tinted forebears wearing antique clothes and serious expressions.

And right in the middle of all these well-loved, familiar faces shine the equally well-loved faces of our friends.

They grin from hasty snapshots, cutting up for the camera or gaping in surprise as the shutter snaps. The snapshots capture the moments, freezing an instant of time.

They smile from formal portraits, carefully posed and lovingly presented. These are the pictures that summarize an era and proclaim, "This is how we looked then."

They cluster in groups, arms around each other, grinning and saying, "Cheese." And they even pull us into the shots, hugging us close, so that our own faces appear smiling among the others in our galleries.

How precious they are to us, these gatherings of faces. Whether they're beautifully framed on a wall, clustered on a table, organized in an album, or even crammed into a box for future sorting, they show where we came from, where we have lived, what we have done. They show our milestones, our memorable occasions. They tell tales of who we have loved, and who has loved us, and how we became who we are. In a sense, they tell the stories of our lives.

And it's fitting that our friends are part of our picture galleries because our friendships also tell the stories of our lives. In a sense, they *are* the story of our lives. Our close relationships reveal the people we are, even as they shape the people we will be. If you really want to know us well, you simply have to take a look at the faces of our friends.

It is in this spirit that the two of us—friends for more than 18 years—have put together this little book on friendship. It was written *by* friends *for* friends—for those who relish and celebrate their special connections and for those who hunger for deeper, better, more meaningful relationships. We want it to be both a celebration of the riches of friendship and a reminder that friendship is a gift we must never take for granted. In this culture where lone-liness and alienation are rampant, we would all do well to cultivate the fine art of making friends and holding fast to the ones we find.

Because this book grew out of our particular friendship, it is partly our own story. But we hope the story it tells is much broader. It is the story of our friends, and of the friends of our friends.

It is also very much the story of the women who have told us about their own precious friendships. We asked women at our conferences to write down some friend-ship stories for us, and the answers they wrote provide a beautiful testament to the power of friendship in people's lives. Theirs are the voices we have quoted in this book under the heading, "A Friendship Story." In sharing all these very personal love stories, we hope we manage to touch on your own story as well, to nudge you into thinking why your friendships are special and to spur you into further action when it comes to cultivating your own friendships.

In particular, this book focuses on women's friend-ships—not because we don't think men can be good friends, but because we believe there is something special about the close friendships we develop with other women. We believe there is a kind of companionship, a kind of understanding, that a woman can only share with another woman. We *need* our girlfriends. We need to reach out to each other and hold each other fast, regardless of what other relationships define our lives.

But this story of friendship is not really a story in the sense that it is an unbroken narrative. It is not a collection of essays or a how-to book. Instead, it strives to tell the story of our lives in the same way that our wall and table galleries tell it: in a varied collection of images. There are a few "portraits" composed as carefully as a studio shot. There are also some informal "snapshots"—friendship stories, how-to lists, even a poem or two.

We've even included some "Something to Ponder" questions for you to answer with your own observations, memories, and thoughts. You might want to record your thoughts about friendship in a journal or, better yet, to write them in a card to one of your dearest friends!

Our hope is that this book will present a beautiful composite picture of the precious gift of women's friendship. As you read it, we hope you will feel blessed, newly thankful for the pleasures and treasures of your friendships. We hope you will feel encouraged and inspired to initiate new friendships and to nurture more lovingly the ones you have. We even have hopes that you might use this book as a tool to build and enhance a treasured friendship. Please make it your own. Write in it. Tuck pictures in it. Use it to remind yourself what your friendships mean or to tell a friend just how much she means to you.

And yes, we know we're not the first friends to write a book on friendship. The bookstore shelves are full of books on friendships in general and women's friendships in particular. Many are quite good. A few are bestsellers. But just as every friendship is unique, and just as there's room in one person's life for more than one friend, we hope this particular book can fill a special niche, helping you to ponder and nurture and celebrate the life-giving connection of one friend to another.

So here it is—our friendship gallery, our gift from friends to friends. If we could summarize its story into one paragraph, it would be this:

Cherish your special friends. Hold them close. Seek them out, enjoy their company, honor them with your care, your energy, and your appreciation. Treasure their faces. And keep them, with sweetest love, in the gallery of your heart.

—*Emilie Barnes*
Riverside, California

—*Donna Otto*
Scottsdale, Arizona

"How can we be so different and
feel so much alike?" mused Flutter.
"And how can we feel so different
and be so much alike?"
wondered Pip. "I think this is
quite a mystery," Flag chirped.
"I agree," said Stellaluna. "But
we're friends. And that's a fact."

—JANELL CANNON,
Stellaluna

1

"Our Friendship Is Like No Other!"

A Picture of a Special Relationship

A faithful friend is a strong defense:
and [she] that hath found such an one
hath found a treasure.

—THE BOOK OF ECCLESIASTES

What Is a Friend?

What is there about a good friend that makes her so special?

Sometimes the simplest answer is the most profound: You like her. You feel better when she's around. You enjoy her company. Her presence refreshes you.

Some friendships are as comforting and comfortable as a well-worn pair of shoes. Others are full of excitement and adventure. The best ones are laced with laughter and softened with tears and strengthened with a spiritual bond.

And here's something else about a friend: You share something in common. It might be a history. It might be a life circumstance. It might be a set of beliefs or a spiritual commitment. It might also be a rhythm, a way of doing things.

13

Whatever it is, when you're with a friend, something feels familiar. You know she is a kindred spirit, a friend of the heart.

A friend is sensitive to the person you are. She listens both to the words you say and to the ones you cannot speak. She *sees* you, and she loves what she sees, and somehow you like yourself better when you're together. With her words and her actions she affirms you, making you feel both loved and lovable. And although you know your friend accepts you just as you are, somehow you know you're better just from being with her.

Your friend sharpens you. She softens you. You *want* to be the person she sees in you.

Trust is the sweet, solid foundation in your relationship with a friend. You trust her to hold close the private things you reveal to her. You trust her to tell you what you need to know, even if the telling is painful, but to tell it gently and discreetly. Your bedrock confidence is that she truly wants the best for you, whatever that best may be.

Day and night, a friend is there for you if you need her. She is willing to give you her time, her energy, her insights, her possessions. She shares the words and the silences. She cries for you and shouts hurrah for you. She is free with her love and her sympathy and her pots of tea and her listening ear.

And yet you don't need to be together every waking moment. You don't have to prove your love and loyalty, even with your time and energy and insight and possessions. There is a freedom in your friendship—a freedom based on a sense of security. You *know* your friend cares about you. You know that even when you're not sure of much else.

And there's something more you know about your friend: Whatever it is she gives to you—whether it's fun or understanding or freedom or trust—you want to give it back to her. The kind of friend she is to you, you want to be for her: loving, giving, trusting, laughing, and crying.

It's not just reciprocity. It's not just payment in kind.

It's the joyful give-and-take of people who love each other and want to be together.

And maybe that's all you really need to make a friend a friend.

Something to ponder . . .

How would I answer the question,
"What is a friend?" . . .

Not a Luxury

They would never actually say it—not in so many words. But some people act as though friendship is somehow frivolous, a luxury they just can't afford.

Despite all the talk about friendship—all the books and cards and gifts that fill the stores, all the songs and television programs about the importance of friends—the feeling still persists that somehow, in this busy world, friendship is optional. That it's a little extra we would love to fit in among all our busy family activities, an indulgence we would really enjoy if we had the time after work.

We know women who think of friendship as something they would really like to be involved in if they have the time. And then they wonder why they're so lonely . . . why they're so stressed . . . why the satisfactions of home and work just don't seem to be enough for them.

We know the reason: It's because they're *not* enough!

The truth is that friendship is anything but luxury. It may be fun, but it's far from frivolous. Our friends are our lifelines, our sanity-savers, our reminders of who we are beyond the roles we play. We may not need our friends to survive (although sometimes it feels that way), but we need them to grow, to be whole, to lead fruitful and productive and satisfying lives.

We need friends to help us through our daily maze of tasks and commitments and involvements.

We need friends to listen to us and talk to us and remind us who we are.

We need friends so we won't be lonely.

And even those of us whose lives are entwined with husbands and children and parents and coworkers know that these in themselves can't keep us from loneliness—unless at least a few of our husbands and children and parents and coworkers become our friends as well. Even then, our outside friends can enrich our family relationships and take a lot of pressure off them.

Friends give us fun and companionship and a sense of being connected to the world. We need that.

Friends help us remember who we are and what we are about in life. They bring us insight and identity. They tell us the truth and challenge us to reach beyond ourselves. We *really* need that.

Friends also give us strength, and we need that perhaps most of all. We need friends to bolster us with words of encouragement, to assure us that we can do what we need to do, to remind us that we're not helpless, to give us a little nudge when we need to move forward. And we need them to move forward with us, to help us do what we couldn't do alone.

We need friends to share the load of living. We were never meant to carry our burdens all by ourselves or to lay them solely on the tender shoulders of the people we live with. We need friends to shore up a corner of our own load when it gets too heavy for us, and we also need the satisfaction and growth that comes from helping friends carry their loads as well.

We need friends for safety. The world can feel treacherous and uncertain. Our footing is surer when we know that someone accepts us as we are, someone has our best interests at heart, someone is always glad to see us, someone plans to stick around.

If we need friends for all these things, why do we persist in living as if friendship were optional? We know better. And we also know, if we'll only admit it to ourselves, that we cannot nurture and develop these friendships that we need unless we make them a priority and set aside time for them.

That's why the two of us have learned to sit down with our calendars and actually schedule times together a year in advance. We live in different cities, and we know that our "friend times" won't happen unless we make time for them.

So each year we block out some time to play together, to talk together, to shop together, just to be together. Each December, as an absolute priority, we set aside a two-day period just for us. The first day is for ourselves—we get a massage or have our nails done or share a long walk. The second day is for our families—we work (and play) together preparing stocking stuffers for the people we love. And the whole time, of course, is good for our souls. It's an annual dose of togetherness that does us both a world of good.

Each year, as well, we look for ways to weave our friendship into the rest of our busy life, so it won't be easy to set it aside. This year we shared Thanksgiving with our families. This year we're writing a book together (this one!). Next year . . . well, we're looking for something.

But it's not easy to carve out this kind of friendship time in the middle of so many other commitments and responsibilities. We're acutely aware of this, and so are you.

Sometimes we feel like we have to scramble for every shared minute. Sometimes we really do have to settle for a phone call and a promise and a grateful prayer that our friend understands how things are—they're the same for her.

But we really can't afford to do it for long.

Friendship isn't caviar and chocolate—delicious, but optional.

It's more like juicy, delicious fruit—flavorful, nutritious, absolutely necessary to healthy, happy living.

Have you had your required daily dose?

Something to ponder . . .

*This is what my special friendships
have done for me . . .*

A Friendship Story

"I met Kitty (Kathryn White) while staying at a beautiful bed and breakfast with my mother who was visiting for the weekend. Kitty was the manager, and since we were her only guests for the evening, we received the royal treatment. Kitty and I ended up sharing our lives and hearts together until two in the morning. It was as if I had known her my whole life! That was over nine years ago, and since then she has played many roles in my life.

"Since there is a thirty-six-year difference, I've realized age isn't a factor in intimate friendships. We share many of the same interests, such as gardening, entertaining, antique collecting, gourmet cooking, bed and breakfasts, tea rooms, traveling, discipling women, and intercessory prayer. God chose Kitty to be an influence in my life and my family's. She is one of my best friends—a kindred spirit, mentor, and mom. She holds us up in prayer with tons of encouragement. She has one of the most gentle and quiet spirits and works harder than anyone I know. When you look into her eyes, you encounter Jesus!"

—Lisa Sears,
Branson, Missouri

Like No Other

We'll never forget the first meal the two of us prepared together. It was a revelation how smoothly and efficiently we meshed. Emilie sliced while Donna diced. Then Donna stirred at the stove while Emilie cleaned the counter. Emilie ran a few inches of suds for washing up as she went along, and Donna knew what it was for—she does it, too.

What a pleasure to be so in sync with another person! We felt as if we had been working together all our lives.

And it's still that way whenever the two of us get in the kitchen. We always feel that sense of wonderment that we are so much alike in the way we cook.

There's just something exhilarating about that feeling of "You're just like me!" It's a feeling of being understood, of being validated, of sharing something special. And it's an important part of what makes us friends.

In our 18 years of friendship, we've discovered so many common qualities that draw us together—some superficial, some very important.

We both grew up in troubled homes, for instance. We both had the responsibility of running the household while our mothers worked. Perhaps because of those childhood lessons, we both value organization and discipline. We share a calling to teach and speak. And now we both work professionally, teaching and speaking about organization! Sometimes we feel that we are the only two people we know who truly understand both the demands of our ministry and our determination to keep it up despite the toll it sometimes takes.

We've both been married many years to the same man. (No, we don't share that much—each of us has her own husband!) And we both spent years as stay-at-home moms, embarking on our present careers only when our nests began to empty. Looking back, we can see that our mothering styles were very similar.

The likenesses go on and on. We both love to cook and entertain. We also, interestingly enough, share a head for business. We do things at similar speeds (fast!), and we share a practical bent that rejoices in results. (Donna's very favorite word is *finished!*)

Most important, perhaps, we share a spiritual commitment and an almost identical set of values. Our Christian faith is important to us. We have a passion for helping women and strengthening families. At heart, we care about the same things, and this commonality bonds us together in a special way.

And yet there are many ways in which we are different.

Donna is taller, with a nose that exuberantly proclaims her Persian/Italian heritage. Emilie is petite, with her father's big brown eyes.

Emilie married her Bob at age 17 and has been married practically all her life. Donna enjoyed a real-estate career in bustling Chicago before she met and married David.

Donna is outspoken and forceful—a quintessential Chicago woman. She has an interest in art and literature and thrives on intellectual and theological debate. Emilie tends to be quieter and more introverted. Though she is a professional speaker, she thinks of herself as more of a homebody and loves nothing better than to putter around the house or play with her grandchildren.

Donna loves the drama and convenience of wearing only black and white. Emilie hates to be tied to any one color scheme.

Donna loves coffee, while Emilie prefers tea.

Emilie actually likes health food. Donna calls it "cardboard."

Donna is funnier and more generous. (Emilie thinks.)

Emilie is sweeter and more patient. (Donna thinks.)

And we are friends, good friends.

Partly it's *because* of our commonalities. We agree on so many important matters. And in our years of friendship we've *created* common ground simply by being together. Our intertwined memories—of days and weeks spent together, gifts and favors exchanged, misunderstandings resolved—

pull us ever closer. We feel a sense of sacredness in what we share together.

But we're also friends in part because of our differences. We complete and balance and intrigue and admire one another. And there's a sense in which we fill each other's special needs.

Emilie has always been drawn to friends who help her loosen up and have fun. She enjoys Donna's ready laugh and playful humor.

Donna has always been drawn to people who offer encouragement, and she thrives on Emilie's nurturing affirmation.

And this doesn't mean that Emilie has no sense of humor and Donna doesn't encourage! It simply means we are friends in part because each of us struggles with something the other person offers easily.

Why does the particular combination work so well?

Who can say for sure?

There really is a certain amount of chemistry in any good friendship, even an element of romance. Some people seem to click, while others don't, and while this is predictable up to a point, it's also a mystery.

From our point of view, at least, it just makes the whole thing more wonderful.

Something to ponder . . .

These are some of the things that tend to attract me in a friend . . .

What do my best friends see in me?

A Friendship Story

"How can two sisters so completely different be such good friends? If someone had told me while I was growing up (I wish they had) that Karen would or could be one of my best friends, I would have said 'No way!' We are so different in many ways, physically and emotionally. Physically, she is golden and fair; I am dark. Karen was always a little more 'filled out,' and I was a tall beanpole. She is quiet and gentle. I speak my mind before thinking about the consequences. Karen is rarely influenced by what others think. I seem to have always had an 'approval addiction.' But the spiritual commonalities we share bring us together.

"I now have two daughters with a son in between just like our parents did. I hope that my daughters can be friends. I know there are hard times, but I want our children to know that our family will always be able to face the things that life brings, together. My sister is one of my very best friends now, and we share so much—one of my favorites is that we sing together. What a blessing to blend with the partner you sing with. But the best thing about my sister is that whenever we talk, we can be honest and open. I have learned from her to speak the truth in love."

—Susan E. Tuten,
Scottsdale, Arizona

My Favorite Things

It's fun to see where friends are different and alike.
What are your favorites?

Donna		Emilie	
book:	anything by Elisabeth Elliot	book:	*Little Women*
movie:	*It's a Wonderful Life*	movie:	*Beaches*
song:	"Be Thou My Vision"	song:	"I Left My Heart in San Francisco"
color:	black and white	color:	blue
movie star:	Jimmy Stewart	movie star:	Harrison Ford
flower:	morning glory or gardenia	flower:	daisy
time of day:	sunset, dusk	time of day:	morning
beverage:	coffee	beverage:	tea
food:	coffee (again!), pasta	food:	Mexican
tree:	carob	tree:	sycamore
season:	winter ("But I live in Phoenix!")	season:	spring

You	*Your Friend*
book:	book:
movie:	movie:
song:	song:
color:	color:
movie star:	movie star:
flower:	flower:
time of day:	time of day:
beverage:	beverage:
food:	food:
tree:	tree:
season:	season:

I "C" You and You "C" Me

Do you realize how many friendship words are "C" words? We started a list for fun, and we were amazed how many there were. Here's our list. Can you think of more?

Commonality	Celebration
Chemistry	Cultivation
(Coffee and Chocolate?)	Connection
Concern	Continuity
Counsel	Cherished Companionship
Courtesy	Cries of Pain
(Keeping) Current	Creative Caring
Contact (Calls and	Communication
Correspondence)	Closeness
Collegiality	Contribution
Catalysts	Chumminess
Caring	Ceremony
Comfort	Consistency

Chocolate, Vanilla, or Butternut Crunch?

Not all friendships are alike, any more than all friends are alike.

Some are casual and relaxing. Others are intense and stimulating.

Some are based on years of shared history. Others are cemented with a single, powerful bond.

Some friendships are intentional, sought-out. Others surprise us, seeming to spring up out of nowhere.

And while some friendships flare and fade, others seem to bud and blossom year after year.

Each individual friendship is as beautifully unique as the two friends who belong to it, and any one person may enjoy a number of beautifully unique friendships.

That's why we're both a little reluctant to talk too much about "best friends." Why is it necessary to rank them on a scale of "good" to "best"? (And is there really such a thing as a "bad" friend?)

We much prefer thinking of our friendships, like ice cream, as coming in a variety of different but delicious flavors.

Some of our friends, for instance, are *everyday friends*. They are the neighbors and colleagues whose company we enjoy on a daily basis. We do favors for each other. We borrow cups of sugar and ballpoint pens and lawn mowers. We swap stories over the back fence or at the watercooler. We are a pleasant part of the fabric of each other's lives. They are our friends.

In addition, most of us enjoy our *specialty friends*—those who share a specialized aspect of our lives. Perhaps we know each other at church. Maybe we play together in a string quartet or chat weekly at the needlework club meeting. Perhaps we have intellectual interests in common and enjoy discussing books and ideas, or maybe we share our needs with one another in a support group. Our contact may be limited to our special-interest gatherings, but these people still play an important role in our lives. They, too, are our friends.

Friends of the memory are those with whom we share a bond because of what has happened in the past. School friends, friends from camp, neighborhood friends from our childhood—we remember them fondly because we became who we are in their company. Although our meetings may be few and far between, we will always consider them our friends.

Touchstone friends are also friends of the memory, but with a special significance. These are the people with whom we touch base regularly, whose lives we follow even though we may not see each other every day or even live close together. We touch base periodically through Christmas cards or letters, phone calls, or regular reunions. These meetings serve the purpose of keeping us grounded, reminding us of who we've been and who we are and also how we've changed. Year after year, we track our growth by connecting to these special friends.

Friends of the moment fill a different place in our lives. These friendships may flare into intimacy because of a common goal or involvement, only to fade away when the project is finished. Or they may grow out of a brief encounter that turns out to have an enormous influence in our life. The closeness we share and our gratitude for the connection are real and vital. We consider these people our friends even if there is no basis for an ongoing relationship.

And then, of course, there are the special friends, the forever friends, the ones we call *friends of the heart.*

Not "true friends," because the other flavors of friendships aren't false.

Not necessarily "best friends," because they don't need to be that exclusive (although there *is* something warm and wonderful about that phrase "best friends"!).

But "friends of the heart" because some unforgettable people, for whatever reason, stake a permanent claim there. These are our chosen sisters—the ones who leave us pondering what we ever did to deserve them.

Best of all, they feel the same way about us.

And that's the most delicious feeling of all.

Friends with Someone You Love

Can a sister be a friend?

Or a mother . . . or daughter?

What about a colleague . . . or a teacher . . . or the woman who grooms your dog?

What about a husband?

Well, you know the answer.

One of the most beautiful things about friendship is that it can transcend categories and roles.

In fact, you never know when a person wearing one role-tag in life—mother, sister, neighbor, child's teacher, pastor's wife, casual acquaintance—might step over the line of labels and sign up as a treasured friend of the heart.

A mentor, for instance, is not necessarily a friend. But a mentor can be a friend.

A coworker is not necessarily a friend. But colleagues do become friends.

A sister is not necessarily a friend. But many sisters are indeed the closest of friends.

Even a husband or boyfriend is not necessarily a friend . . . although there is a special joy in building a friendship with your mate or potential mate. And it's a fortunate woman who has the privilege of calling her mother—or her daughter—a friend of her heart.

For Emilie, experiencing this transformation with her daughter, Jenny, has been a bright spot of gold in years filled with darkness. In the crucible of family crisis and serious illness, she and Jenny have come to know and trust each other more deeply than they ever imagined. They have talked more honestly, cared for each other more mutually, learned more about support and forgiveness than they would ever have guessed.

Does this always happen between mothers and daughters . . . or sisters . . . or colleagues . . . or any two people whose lives are linked for other reasons?

You already know this answer, too.

There is a mystery to the ways of friendship. Even when two people are willing, it doesn't always happen. Sometimes one or both are not willing, or don't know how.

That's not even bad. You can have fruitful relationships with those who are not your close friends—especially those you care about as family members.

But when you do see a door to friendship open with someone who is already in your life, we urge you to consider stepping through.

Finding a friend is like discovering treasure.

Finding a friend in someone you already love—that's like finding a treasure in the rafters of your very own attic.

A Friendship Story

"Isn't it sheer joy to know you have a friend who shares your heart? Though my friend and I are very different in appearance and 15 years span our ages, we've been pals for over 40 years. We've been blessed to share most of the important events of our lives together, and we've learned to treasure our differences over the years.

"While I feel most uncomfortable meeting people, her gentle, graceful style puts people right at ease. She artfully has even passing acquaintances sharing personal stories and feeling they have made a friend after only a brief encounter. (Knowing her has not only enriched my life, but taught me some valuable lessons as well.) . . . Quite wise, she is amazingly forgiving of my sometimes loud, less than genteel remarks; gently reminding me of a calmer, softer side I could not see. Even when living sometimes 500 miles apart, we sense how the other is, just as if the bond we share is unaffected by physical bounds.

"One Christmas, joyously anticipating my friend's arrival, I bought her a beautiful tapestry pillow. . . . It would be so pretty in her living room, and I just knew she would love it. After the gift was wrapped, I couldn't stop thinking it would be beautiful in *my* house, too. So the gift volleyed from the tree to the closet until the day my special friend arrived. When she presented me with an ornately wrapped box, I gave her the prized pillow gift. As I began to unwrap, she said, 'You know, I almost didn't give this present to you. I must admit I wanted to keep it for myself.' As we tore through paper and ribbon, we both held up the same pillow! After the laughter and tears subsided, we both agreed we gave the gift because we loved each other. I would expect nothing less from my special friend. After all, she gave me life. She is my mother. And she is the greatest of friends."

Melissa J. Garner,
Little Rock, Arkansas

Not a Friend

There's a difference between being friendly to others and being close friends with everyone. One you can do, or at least aspire to. The other is simply impossible.

We human beings aren't made to be intimate companions with the whole human race. That's an insight that mostly comes with maturity. Friendship is a precious thing to be guarded and valued, not carelessly dispensed nor cavalierly treated.

It's important to remember, too, that not everyone is a friend who claims to be one.

The waiter who gives us his name and insists on engaging us in conversation—he's not necessarily our friend.

The airplane seatmate who tells us the story of her life— she's not necessarily our friend.

The telemarketer who chats amiably before settling down to her spiel—she's almost certainly not our friend.

But these are superficial examples, minor annoyances.

More problematic is the colleague who invites our confidences, then spreads them behind our backs. More troubling is the acquaintance who claims to love us dearly but consistently forgets our birthday and can't keep our children straight and just doesn't have time to help when we have a problem. More disturbing is the associate who always needs to talk but never can manage to listen.

These people are not true friends of any flavor. Anyone who takes her friendships seriously would be wise to guard against these kinds of false friendships.

A false friend is not just a friend who hurts us. Most friends manage to hurt and betray each other from time to time—that's why forgiveness is essential to any lasting friendship.

A false friend is something different. She is one who, for whatever reason, just doesn't have our best interest at heart, but who tries to hide her chronic ill will behind loving words and friendly gestures. Or she is one whose own self-centeredness makes her incapable of the give-and-take of friendship. Her path may parallel yours. You may run in the same circles and have civil exchanges, but the qualities of a true, intimate friendship—trust, openness, honesty, mutual caring—are just not there.

Sometimes a false friend is easy to recognize. Other times you don't have a clue until you find you've been betrayed. But it helps to keep your eyes open, especially to the way your friend treats others. (If she talks behind another person's back, who's to say she won't talk behind yours?) You usually can trust your instincts. If you feel uneasy in her company, perhaps there's a reason. You can remind yourself that true friendship is something that must be earned, and you don't owe everyone the gift of your friendship.

That is an important thing to keep in mind, although many people misunderstand.

It is important to be kind and polite to whomever crosses our path. It's important to show love and compassion to people in need. But it is simply folly to accept everyone as a true friend.

We can learn from false friends—especially lessons in how *not* to treat people.

We can even feel for them, for false friends are often people in pain.

But we don't have to give them our trust.

We don't even have to give them much of our time.

We don't have to hold them close to our hearts.

It's one thing to be friendly.

But it's simply not necessary—nor is it wise—to be everyone's friend.

True friends are too precious for us to squander our trust and our time on those whose friendship is false.

Beautiful Music Together

What a delight to learn something new about an old friend!

Even more delightful is to discover something the two of us have had in common all along . . . and never knew till now.

That's how we felt on the afternoon when we found out we had both played the cello as girls.

"You're kidding! You, too?"

"I can't believe it."

Neither of us was first-chair material, and neither of us has held a bow in many a year. But we both dearly loved the process of making music on that wonderful, mellow instrument. And we both were thrilled to be involved in the creation, however imperfect, of something truly beautiful.

The more we thought about it, in fact, the more we realized that's exactly what we're doing as we live and share as friends.

We're collaborating on a lovely, joyful, unique work of art.

If our friendship were music, it would be a wonderful duet—a composition for four hands.

If it were a painting, it would be a collaborative canvas—a landscape colored with dual brushes.

If it were a tapestry, it would be woven with two dancing shuttles—the threads of our days and moments and our single and shared threads combining to create surprising and unforgettable patterns.

We don't want to go overboard with the metaphors here! But the point is that all friendship is a joint creation—a beautiful thing we create over time, together.

We craft it from the simplest materials: our words and our silences and our silliness and our sacrifice and our gifts and our gestures. And we take turns sounding the notes and wielding the brush and weaving the thread.

You give. I take. Then we switch places.

There are some times when you take the lead, other times when I do. Sometimes we plan where our collaboration is going; other times we improvise joyfully.

I invite you to come visit me, and we share a cup of tea.

You tell a funny story. I listen and laugh. Then I tell one.

I see you are hurting and try to help. You hear my need and send me an encouraging note.

You counsel my children. I hold you up in prayer.

That's the way it goes: One mellow note, then another answering. One stroke of color, then another beside it. A change of thread, a sweep of the shuttle.

Bit by bit, something lovely is created, and most of the time it doesn't even feel like work. Often it feels like fun. And almost always, even in the midst of trouble, there's a sense of elation.

It's a joy to create something beautiful. And it's a joy to be part of a miracle—because all intimate friendships, like all works of true art, have a bit of the miraculous about them.

Maybe it's because we know that this beautiful thing we created together is somehow more than we are.

Maybe our enthusiastic brush strokes have been touched up while we slept.

Maybe our dancing shuttles have been guided by a Master Weaver.

Maybe our mellow duet has been a trio all along—with the true Source of these heavenly harmonies!

We think so, anyway. Because we know this work of art that is our friendship is far more beautiful than anything the two of us second-chair friends could manage!

Something to ponder . . .

To me, my most treasured friendships
can be compared to . . .

20 Questions (to Ask a Friend)

These questions provide a fun forum for getting to know your new friends and getting to know your old friends better. Use them for party games, for conversation starters. For an old and treasured friend, see how many you can guess about her!

1. Where did your family live when you were six? When you were 12?
2. What was your favorite subject in school?
3. Have you ever played a musical instrument? What was it?
4. What is your favorite sport? Did you ever play it—or did you prefer to watch?
5. What was your least favorite food as a child?
6. Name your first boyfriend. How old were you when you met?
7. If you were beginning life again and could choose any career, what would you choose?
8. What is the most valuable thing you've learned in the past ten years?
9. What lost person or thing in your life do you miss the most?
10. What is the most encouraging word anyone can say to you?
11. Describe the most wonderful vacation you've ever taken. Why was it so great?
12. In what areas of your life do you feel most successful? Least successful?
13. What was the loneliest moment of your life? Why?
14. What single accomplishment in your life have you been proudest of?
15. What is your favorite season of the year and why?
16. Name an older person (not your parents) who influenced you as a younger person.
    What did you learn from that person?
17. If you had an unlimited budget to remodel just one room in your house, what would you do? In which room?
18. What was your favorite song when you were 16?
19. If you had to spend a year alone on a desert island and could take just three things with you, what would you take?
20. What's your idea of a truly perfect morning? What would you do?

𝒾❤ 𝒾❤ 𝒾❤

"You must be a friend," said Corduroy.
"I've always wanted a friend."
"Me too!" said Lisa, and
gave him a big hug.

—DON FREEMAN,
Corduroy

𝒾❤ 𝒾❤ 𝒾❤

2

"Remember When We Met?"

How Friendships Get Started

"A [woman] that hath friends must
show [herself] friendly."

—THE BOOK OF PROVERBS

Once Upon a Time

All stories have to begin somewhere. And
so all friendships have their tales of "how
we got together in the first place."

Sometimes the beginnings are murky, shrouded in child-hood mists or simply faded in the distance. Some friends can't recall a time when they weren't together.

But often the stories of our beginnings are clear and vivid—memory milestones. And just as children cherish the stories of their birth as reminders of how valued they are in a family, we think friends ought to cherish the tales of their beginnings. These tales are fun to tell, and valuable because they remind us of why we're friends in the first place.

Not every friendship story begins with "once upon a time." Every beginning is different, as unique as the friendship, although most tales of beginning do follow a familiar path.

First there's a meeting: "Once upon a time there were two people." Usually it's face-to-face—an introduction, a chance encounter, or simply finding yourself in the same place at the same time. Friendships begin in grade-school classrooms, in workplace restrooms, in church nurseries, in soccer-field bleachers. It's possible to meet by telephone (we did) or by mail or even by reputation ("You really need to meet so-and-so; I just know you would love each other").

Once you've met, in order for an encounter to develop into a friendship, somebody has to reach out, to take the next step. It could be as simple as a question that sparks a conversation or a compliment that warms a heart:

> "Do you have any other children?"
> "Where did you grow up?"
> "I really admire your work on that sampler."

Or it could be an invitation:

> "Would you like to have lunch with me tomorrow?"
> "A group of us likes to go to this antique shop. Would you like to come?"
> "Want to grab a cup of coffee and talk?"

And then, if the friendship is going to work, the other person has to respond with some kind of a yes. Not perhaps to a specific question or invitation, but yes to the possibility of friendship.

Next comes one of the most fun parts in a beginning friendship. Remember that charming little song from *The King and I*, "Getting to Know You"? That's what you're doing in those days when you are exchanging stories and discovering each other.

It's almost like a courtship—a little dance. It's a series of offers and responses, of questions and answers, of give-and-take. With every interaction you are learning "beautiful and new" things about one another.

Then one day, at some point along the way, you realize that your "once upon a time" has launched itself into a full-fledged tale of friendship.

Now, some stories start right at the beginning, while others meander into the heart of the tale at a leisurely pace. And that's true of friendships, too.

Sometimes the "getting to know you" period is so abbreviated you almost don't know it's there. You have the sense that you were friends from the moment you met . . . or even before.

Other times, the courtship is prolonged—you remain for days or months or years as colleagues or casual acquaintances or people who once met or people who like each other but somehow can't manage to get together. And then one day, for some reason, you click. You start talking and you can't stop. Or you run into each other at your child's ball game and have such a fabulous time sitting together that you can't understand why you didn't get together before. Or you happen to share a crisis or a challenge that throws you together and draws you close.

It doesn't really matter how or when it happens. It's the variations in the story that make it so interesting and wonderful. It's the twists and turns that make the story worth telling.

But you know when you've reached the heart of the story! A spark has fired and it's lit a warm fire in your hearts, and you're beginning to enjoy and to trust and to love each other, and something tells you this is going to last awhile.

And then you can begin looking back together and telling each other, "Remember when it first began?"

A Friendship Story

"When my best friend, my life partner for 12 years, died suddenly and unexpectedly at age 54, I turned to the Internet for support. I dropped into the family forum on CompuServe and found a few others to communicate with. A few weeks later a cry of help from a 'new widow' appeared.

"We wrote back and forth sharing our stories—her husband had had a heart attack at his daughter's wedding—and our feelings. We sent each other pictures of ourselves and our spouses. We became the single most important support person for each other during the very difficult grieving process, and we are still in touch today. We wrote notes daily until recently and now write several times a week; the record serves as my journal. It's been almost two years.

"We have never met. I live in Oregon and she lives in Eastern Canada. Despite that, I know I have made a special friend for life, and we know as much about each other as our local friends do. I wouldn't be the same without her."

—Sally J. Mann,
Eugene, Oregon

You Never Know

Our own story started with friends of friends.

A woman Emilie knew in Riverside kept mentioning that *her* friend in Arizona knew someone Emilie would really like.

And a friend of Donna's in Phoenix kept talking about this great woman in California that a friend of hers had met.

"You've got so much in common."

"I know you would just love each other!"

"You really ought to call."

The problem was: we just weren't all that interested!

Each of us had too much going on in her life (we thought) to worry about making friends with a woman who lived in a completely different state and had a completely different life.

But Emilie's friend kept talking to Donna's friend. And those friends kept urging us to get together. And finally one of us made the phone call.

It was fine. We enjoyed the conversation. And that was that. Remember, we really didn't have time to worry about making friends with a woman who lived in a completely different state and had a completely different life.

Except one phone call led to another. And we discovered we really did have a lot in common. And after a fair number of long-distance phone calls we even began to wonder if we should work together. At that time Emilie's home-management business was really beginning to take off and she was considering selling franchises. Perhaps Donna should take over a franchise.

So Donna flew to Riverside to meet Emilie and sit in on a seminar. And we talked a lot. We found out we really liked each other, although we still didn't know if the franchise idea would work.

Well, the upshot was that the franchise idea *didn't* work, but the friendship did. Today the two of us enjoy separate (though similar) careers, but our lives are anything but separate. We've decided we just can't afford not to be friends. And even though we live in completely different states, we have managed to keep a lively friendship going for more than 18 years.

When did we know it was going to happen?

As we remember, it was really two different moments.

For Emilie, it happened on Donna's first visit, when Donna sat down and spelled out, "This is what I do: A, B, C." Emilie thought, *I like this person. She's really organized. And I can't believe she took the trouble to come all the way out here and talk to me.*

For Donna, it came a little later, while we were still negotiating about the possibility of a franchise. Donna asked a very pointed question: "What if I go with you now but later on I decide to branch out and hold seminars on my own?" Emilie's answer was that that would be fine—there's plenty of room out there for both of us. And Donna remembers thinking, *I like this person. I can't believe she's so generous and gracious.*

By that time, we were well on the way to becoming close friends.

And what did we learn from the unusual start of our story?

Simply that it's a good idea to keep your eyes and heart open . . . because you never know where your next close friend is coming from!

Beginning Stories

*I*n many ways," writes Sharon J. Wohlmuth in the introduction to her book *Best Friends* "[friendship] is all the more precious because something so powerful can spring from origins as elusive as a chance meeting or a shared interest." Here are some stories our friends have told us of how they met. How did your most treasured friendships start?

- ❧ Emilie met her friend Barbara D. Lorenzo while delivering product from a home business. Something about Barbara's house caught Emilie's eye, and she thought, *I could like a person who lives in that house.*

- ❧ Donna met her friend Sandy when they both agreed to be part of a friendship covenant group. They met at the very first group meeting, and Sandy's still a treasured friend.

- ❧ Marilyn and Linda were introduced by Linda's real-estate agent right after Linda moved to town. They bonded at first because they were Midwesterners transplanted into a Southwestern town, then discovered mutual interests in cooking, antiques, and the arts. But it was nine years of sharing a daily walk (and drinking coffee) that really cemented their friendship.

- ❧ Anne met Debra working after hours at work. Debra had just been hired and was putting her new office together. Anne was plugging away at her desk when Debra came foraging for a hammer. The best Anne could do was a stapler . . . but the friendship has held together fine!

❧ Maxine was surprised to become friends at work with a woman she had known from a distance in high school—a woman she had always thought of as an unapproachable "popular person." All it really took was a chance to talk together outside of their previous roles. Then they discovered they shared a spiritual commitment and an interest in writing. They've been friends ever since.

Something to ponder . . .

If I were to write a story of how a special friendship began, this is how it would go . . .

L♥ L♥ L♥

A Friendship Story

"When I was in fifth grade, I met my best friend Victoria. She and I were both recently fatherless, shy, and nonremarkable in many ways. As the years passed, we grew in the most beautiful friendship and sisterhood. We shared everything together: secrets, crushes on boys, our insecurities, and all manner of secrets that young women share. . . . Truly God used us to help each other grow, not only in our youth, but in spiritual matters as well. As the years passed, our friendship thrived through our teen years, and beyond to our twenties. We both wound up living in Vancouver, Washington, at the same time with our spouses and families. I saw her on a regular basis.

"When we were 28 (17 years after we met), Victoria died suddenly from a pulmonary embolism on Easter morning. For several years, I wondered how I could survive without her friendship, but her mark is as strong on my soul now as it was in our childhood. I still hear her in my memories and in my heart, loving, understanding, and encouraging me to be that person that God made and intended me to be. She will never be on this earth again, but this makes my home-coming to heaven all the sweeter, as I not only will see my Lord, but my dearest friend as well."

—Carol Ann Hickman,
Junction City, Oregon

L♥ L♥ L♥

Choosing or Chosen?

Do you choose your friendships—or do your friendships choose you?

It's probably a little bit of both—or it should be.

Sometimes it does feel like you were destined to be together, that you are instant friends with someone without having anything to say in the matter. It's almost as if God chose the two of you to be together and gave you your friendship as a gift. But you still chose to say yes to the friendship, to invest your time and energy toward nurturing it.

Sometimes, on the other hand, you feel like one of you is the chooser and the other is the chosen. In fact, most friendships begin, we believe, when one person chooses to pursue the other as a friend. In our friendship it was Donna who took the initiating role. But both of us have played chooser and chosen roles in friendships. At times we have switched roles within our own relationship.

There's always an element of choice in making and keeping friends. And just as your mother probably told you, it's vitally important to choose the right friends.

Now, some people really resist this idea. To them, choosing friends sounds somehow elitist, as if you were gazing down your nose from Mount Olympus and selecting those people who are good enough to associate with or picking the winner at a beauty contest or squeezing all the cantaloupes in the market to find the ripest one.

But that's not really what choosing friends mean. It's not a matter of judging people, then picking some and rejecting the others. We all have met plenty of perfectly splendid persons who for one reason or another didn't become our close friends.

The way we see it, choosing friends is simply part of being responsible human beings. It's part of facing the reality that our time and our energy—even our stay on this earth—is finite, and that investing it wisely means learning to focus. Trying to spread ourselves among too many people almost inevitably means developing deep, intimate relationships with none. So it makes sense to choose to spend time with relationships that truly nourish the souls of both of you.

Choosing friends, then, is also a part of knowing ourselves, realizing that certain associations strengthen us, teach us, and fill our needs, while others push our buttons or feed our weaknesses. It's part of caring for ourselves, realizing that we really do need the support of those who share our values and "fill our cups."

All this means that it's a good idea to have a picture of what is important to you in a friend. It helps to know what you can live with and what you can't, what's really important to you and what you can let slide.

It's not elitist to face the fact that lazy people tend to drive you crazy, or that loud people make you cringe, or that you just can't trust someone who can't remember your birthday. (Someone else may actually prefer a friend who is less driven, more enthusiastic, who doesn't follow the rules.)

It's not elitist to realize that a chronic complainer tends to bring out the whine in you, too. (Someone else might easily be able to resist the whine while enjoying the generosity and genuine thoughtfulness that go along with that particular complainer.)

It's certainly not elitist to realize that hanging out with compulsive shoppers tends to wreak havoc with your budget resolves! Sometimes you simply have to recognize your limits.

Remember, when you choose your friends, you're not choosing whom you will talk to, whom you will associate with, whom you will reach out to or help or show kindness to.

You're deciding whom you will trust with your heart and your soul.

You're deciding who will work with you as you try to accomplish what you were put on earth to do.

You're deciding who can handle and accept and love the you beneath the surface.

And it's a simple fact that not everyone qualifies for that very specialized position, just as you may not be qualified to fill it in some people's lives.

But lest this sound too heavy, remember that you're almost never required to make these choices all at once. Usually you make a series of small choices that lead you down the path toward friendship. And usually there are plenty of opportunities along the way to back out if you feel the friendship simply isn't working.

Here's how it typically goes:

First, you choose, consciously or unconsciously, to open your mind to the possibility of a friendship.

Then you choose to take the next step. You smile. You say hello. You respond. And then you make the phone call or issue the invitation, and the other person reciprocates.

With each step you are choosing to move forward with the friendship or to pull away.

And here's the really good news.

You have the opportunity all your life to continue to choose loving, supportive, trustworthy friends. You even have the opportunity to change your mind, to decide that the quality you just can't live with is overshadowed by an even more sterling quality you just can't live without.

And the best part of all is realizing your friend feels the same about you.

After all, she chose you as a friend.

Finding Friends

There are times in our lives when choosing friends seems less of an issue than finding them in the first place.

These are usually the transition times. Maybe you've moved to a new house or a new town or even across the country. Or maybe you've been widowed or divorced or your children have grown and you've changed jobs. Whenever you pass a milestone or go through a change, you might find that you have less in common with your old friends, or that they're just too far away to come over on the spur of the moment to share a cup of tea and a good cry.

Those can be lonely times—those days when you're feeling short of friends. You really feel the lack of someone to shop with, someone to chat over the fence with, someone to call for a lunch date. You feel a little awkward starting over again with people who don't know you from Eve.

But here's the good news: These lonely times can also be growing times. They're times of opportunity and promise, when new acquaintances can add freshness to your life. You can reinvent yourself as you develop new relationships. You can look back over your past and perhaps correct old mistakes. You can practice faith and patience, because you really can't hurry the natural process of getting to know others.

And you can remember (for this is true) that the lonely times usually don't last.

In the meantime, there are some things you can do to make it all a little easier.

First of all, make use of your lifelines. These are the ties you still maintain: your friends from your previous job, your long-time friends who live far away, your family, your dog. This is not the time in your life to worry about the phone bill.

This is not the time to hole up and hide. Write letters. Keep up contact with the people who love you, even if they don't fill your need for close-up friends. Solicit their prayers. Ask them to visit. If at all possible, arrange to make your own visits.

Second (this is the obvious one) take steps to put yourself in friendship's way. Consider joining organizations, volunteering for jobs, pursuing interests you might not have pursued before. It's hard to make new friends while you're sitting at home.

Third, try to reach out. If you meet someone you like, make a friendly overture. Smile or say hello. Ask her to lunch. Invite her to go somewhere with you. When someone else speaks to you, respond. Say yes when you can. Give yourself a chance to get to know the other person.

It helps to open your mind to friendship possibilities you might not have considered. A friend doesn't have to be someone just like you. In fact, some of our most fulfilling, enduring friendships have been with someone who is older . . . or younger . . . or from a different walk in life.

A stay-at-home mom can be friends with a mother who works outside the home. A Ph.D. really can resonate with a high-school graduate if you have other things in common. An older widow who lives alone can develop a fulfilling friendship with the young couple across the street.

So don't limit yourself as you look for friends. Say hello to someone who appeals to you, even if she's not what you've always considered "friend material." You never know who might turn out to be your next bosom buddy.

And here's something we've found to be very helpful in those transitional, low-friend times. When you find yourself short on intimate nearby friends, try to make a point of being thankful for what you do have.

For instance, you can say thank you for any companionship, even if it doesn't blossom into full-fledged friendship.

Not all your encounters will click, but it's still nice to have someone to run with or drink coffee with or talk to in class. Besides, you never know what future friendships will spring from present acquaintances.

You can also say thank you for the free time that a shortage of friends may bring. This can be a time to explore your own heart, to read and learn something new, to enjoy those interests that your former friends might not have shared. Now is a time to reflect on the kind of friend you've been in the past and resolve to be a better friend in the future. Chances are, your life will soon be filled once again with the privileges and obligations of friendship. Now is a time to enjoy the quiet.

You can even say thank you, as well, for the empty space that has opened up in your life. It may not feel like a blessing, but it very well might be. Perhaps that space is there for a purpose—it's waiting to be filled by a future friend of the heart. So instead of rushing to fill the friendship void in your life, you might try leaving it open for a little while. Think of it as leaving room for future friendships God has in mind for you.

Then wait. Pray. Hold onto your lifelines and put yourself in friendship's way, but don't push too hard. Practice trusting that you'll be granted the friendship you need when you need it.

Believe it.

You will.

Where to Meet Friends

❧ on a bench at the playground

❧ at an elderhostel

❧ in a choir

❧ at the library

❧ at church

❧ at a museum

❧ at a committee meeting

❧ in the break room at work

❧ at a softball game

❧ at a Bible study or study group

❧ in the produce department of the grocery store

❧ on the beach

❧ at a prayer group

❧ at a pottery studio

❧ at another friend's house

What to Do with a New Friend

✍ exercise

✍ go to a movie

✍ shop

✍ clean house together

✍ meet for coffee or tea

✍ take a walk in the park

✍ visit a day spa

✍ pray

✍ read and discuss a book

✍ browse for books or antiques

✍ share a picnic

✍ take the kids on an outing

A Friendship Story

"Having heart-to-heart friendships has always been very important to me. I have been truly blessed as each friendship has grown over time, through various trials. So when we had to move away from our lifelong home-town, it was difficult to think of leaving my friends and having the energy to cultivate new ones.

"On our first house hunting visit to the new area, we attended church on Sunday. There I met a warm and friendly woman named Fran. . . . She gave me names and information, including her name and phone number. Somehow when she said to call her if I needed anything, I sensed she really meant it.

"In the months before we actually moved, I contacted her a couple more times, we met at lunch, and we both felt a special bond of friendship already growing. She showed up at our house the day we moved in and was a tremendous practical support to me in the first weeks as I needed help in a totally new environment. Although we only lived there eight months, our husbands also became friends. I was amazed at how the Lord blessed us with such a 'fast' friendship.

"I am glad I had the courage to reach out in my time of need, and I thank God for sending a warm hand to take hold of mine. It takes two!"

—Cathie McCormick,
Venetia, Pennsylvania

"I Have All the Friends I Need"

In a sense, you can't ever have too many friends.

But both of us have had times in our lives when our hearts felt closed to the possibility of new involvements.

Sometimes we've felt like we didn't have enough time or energy for anyone outside our families and our work and our small circle of old friends.

Other times we were grieving the deeply felt loss of a good friend, and something in us rebelled at the idea of filling up her place.

Have you ever felt that way—as if your heart was just too full for one more good friend?

Well, there's wisdom, of course, in knowing your limits.

But there's also wisdom in keeping a corner of your heart open to the new.

Maybe we believe this because our own friendship started in one of those too-full times. What a shame it would have been to miss this relationship just because our lives were so full!

But how do you keep your heart open when it wants to be closed?

We've found that it helps to keep an open-ended view of life—remembering that every life is an unfinished painting until the final brush strokes are taken. You still don't know all the major elements that will form the composition of your life.

You're still in progress, and there will be changes. And the relationships that call to you today may well be the ones that carry you through the next phase of development.

An unfinished painting is far more evocative and haunting than a finished one. Something in that empty space—the areas that are sketched but not colored, or blocked in but not finished—speaks of possibilities and promise.

When you look at your life that way—as still in progress, not as sewn-up and unchangeable—you'll find your heart stays more open to new friendships.

And when you do that . . . you'll find that new possibilities are always right around the corner.

Connecting . . . 18 Great Ideas for Meeting New Friends and Getting to Know Them Better

Whether you're a newcomer or an old hand, these ideas can help you connect with potential friends.

1. *Carry a card.* Keep a small supply of business cards or personal calling cards in your purse. That way, if you meet a new friend, it's easy to say, "Call me." Don't forget to jot down the new friend's name and number on another card for you to keep.

2. *Drop a line.* Keep a little basket of note cards or postcards, a pen, and some stamps in a convenient spot. If you meet someone you would like to know better, drop her a note and tell her so. If you have a computer, send off a quick e-mail.

3. *Issue an invitation.* The only way to get past the level of small talk is to schedule some time together. Invite a new acquaintance to lunch, to tea, or just to share a coffee break. Or invite her along on a shopping trip or an afternoon workout.

4. *Give a compliment.* When you see something you like, develop the habit of saying so. Nothing warms the heart of a potential friend like feeling appreciated.

5. *Take notes.* If you're reaching the age where you tend to forget details, actually write down important things you learn about a new acquaintance: her husband's name, her birthday, her children's ages, where she lived before.

6. *Offer a welcome.* It's hard to move into a new community or area. If someone new moves into your neighborhood, community, or church, take a minute for an

old-fashioned gesture of welcome. A basket full of maps, coupons, and treats speaks a wonderful welcome, but even a store-bought pie or a plate of bakery cookies can break the ice and jump-start friendship.

7. *Open your mind.* Your next best friend just might be someone you don't expect—perhaps someone older, younger, or simply different.

8. *If you click, connect.* Sometimes you'll find yourself striking up a conversation with a stranger in the beauty shop, in the grocery store line, or at the playground. Don't let that potential friend walk away! Ask her to go for a cup of coffee, or exchange phone numbers or e-mail addresses.

9. *Leave room in your life for future friends.* Try scheduling some things to do alone on a regular basis—a walk in the neighborhood, an hour in the garden, a moment for tea—with the idea that you might share that time later with a new friend.

10. *Introduce friends to friends.* Your circle of friends is bound to enlarge, and you may meet some special new people in the process. In fact, why not throw a party and ask each guest to bring a friend from a different walk of life?

11. *Learn something new.* Take a class, buy a how-to book, join a study group, contact an expert who knows something you want to know. The more you ask questions and participate in your new interest, the more potential friends you're apt to meet.

12. *Nourish spiritual connections.* Attend worship, or join a study or prayer group. If you meet someone who seems to share your interest in spiritual matters, ask if she would consider sharing with you on a regular basis.

13. *Join a group, or start one.* One of the best ways to meet friends is to join a group of people you have something in common with: a "Mommy and Me" group, a quilter's guild, a rock collector's meeting. How do you find a group? Look in the newspaper, ask at the public library, inquire at shops (a needlework shop might host a needlework group), or surf the net (a national organization might list a local meeting). If you can't find a group, post a message on a bulletin board to find someone who might be interested in starting one with you.

14. *Build on common ground.* If you meet someone whose circumstances or interests are similar to yours, suggest pooling resources. Perhaps you could clean house together (half the time at each house), share yard work, walk your dogs together, or gather all the kids into one yard for games and conversation. You'll take care of necessary tasks while building a relationship.

15. *Ask for help with a project.* It's not only a good way to get the job done; it's also a nice way to get to know someone better.

16. *Offer someone a ride* to a meeting or other gathering. The gesture is usually appreciated, and the commute is a nice time to get to know each other better.

17. *Make friends on the job.* Working together is a great way to make new friends, and this is true whether the job is a volunteer committee spot or a full-time career. If you find yourself low on friends and you have the time, consider getting a job of some kind. Then if you "click" with a coworker, ask her to share a cup of coffee or an off-duty dinner.

18. *Keep a yes in your heart.* You never know whether the next person you meet will turn out to be a dear chosen sister.

ℒ ℒ ℒ

*"I'll talk all day if you'll
only set me going. Beth says
I never know when to stop."*

—Louisa May Alcott,
Little Women

ℒ ℒ ℒ

3

"I Always Laugh When I'm with You"

On Being Together

"But it was you . . . my companion. . . .
We took sweet counsel together."

—THE BOOK OF PSALMS

Playing Together

"Can you come out and play?"

Remember when those were the words you wanted most to hear?

When we were little, after all, the central purpose of having friends was having someone to play with.

Our play was really our work, of course. It was the way we learned. But oh, how we loved to do it together: riding bikes, jumping rope, dressing our dolls, playing make-believe.

Remember what it was like to play with your friends?

You still need that feeling in your life.

You need fun in your friendships, for that quality of play is what lifts you and renews you and refreshes you. You need friends to go to movies with (especially the ones your husband or male friend just won't go to), to shop garage sales with, to share cookouts with your family, to talk with on the phone, or just to sit with and enjoy a beautiful afternoon and a cup of tea and some laughter.

Maybe not every friend is a fun friend. Some friendships seem to exist just to share adversity. And certainly a sturdy friendship will have far more to it than shared amusement. But the deepest friendships, as far as we've been able to tell, are almost always fertilized by fun. Almost always, friends of the heart are friends who play together.

What you do for fun, of course, will depend on who you are together, what interests you share. It will depend on what you need, what diversions bring you relaxation and joy . . . certainly on what the two of you have in common.

Some friends play games. Donna's sweet mother-in-law had a group of friends—they called themselves "the girls"— who met in kindergarten and grew up together and then met regularly for bridge games until Mom moved to Arizona at age 76. Those friends and games were a support group, a source of therapy as well as fun for all those years.

Other friends love to share physical activity: tennis or racquetball or mall-walking or bungee jumping. (Whether this is fun or not will depend on your point of view, but even shared misery can be a great friendship-builder!) The two of us have always loved to share walks when we're together— talking nonstop or just enjoying each other's companionship as we walk the canal path beneath the orange blossoms in Riverside or hike up into Phoenix's red desert mountains.

Some friends have fun sharing hobbies: decorating, needlework, pottery, even woodworking. (We like to cook and read magazines and go to movies and go antiquing.) Some friends make music together . . . or create new recipes together . . . or play games with the children or grandchildren . . . or garden side by side.

Some friends share adventures and collect stories for future telling, like the time Emilie and her friend Yoli decided to take Yoli's husband's kayak out on the bay in Newport Beach. They were not the best and most experienced of rowers, and they spent most of that outing going backwards. But when they were through, they pulled the kayak up on the shore and lay down and just laughed and laughed.

And laughter is surely a healing, restorative part of the fun that comes with friendship. Our best friends, we find, are the ones we can laugh with. It's the laughter that lubricates our irritations, that releases our tensions, that feeds our joy. Whether it comes from gentle teasing (Emilie's husband, Bob, and Donna love to rib each other!) or funny anecdotes or cartoons clipped from the paper or just silliness and giggles . . . it's the laughter that helps keep things warm and joyful, even in the midst of pain.

Celebration, too, is part of the fun. Celebrating milestones. Celebrating accomplishments. Celebrating the fact that it's a beautiful day and you are friends. Whether you are a party person or you prefer quieter ceremonies of rejoicing, you feed your friendships with fun whenever you stage a celebration. That's why we recommend, whenever possible, that you celebrate extravagantly and enthusiastically. Bring out the balloons and the confetti. Deliver solemn speeches and lots of hugs. Wear silly hats.

Silliness, as a matter of fact, adds a special quality to the fun in any friendship. That's because it takes a lot of trust to let down your guard and be truly silly, even with someone you love. You're letting yourself be a child again, and trusting your child-self to another person. When you feel free to act absolutely silly with a friend, you understand most fully the freedom a friendship can grant.

Have you ever grabbed a friend and gone to the park to swing?

Or shared impersonations of people you both know?

Or sat down on the floor with a bunch of coloring books and colored to your heart's content?

Or bought yourself a balloon to carry through the mall?

Count yourself blessed if you have a friend who doesn't mind—or, even better, wants to do it with you.

For that matter, you should count yourself blessed for all the fun you have with any of your friends.

For fun isn't frivolous, any more than play is frivolous for a child.

Fun is an important reward of friendship.

It's part of the gift you give each other—the gift of abundant joy.

Friends Share . . .

❧	recipes	❧	chores
❧	beauty tips	❧	phone calls
❧	exercise	❧	clothes (sometimes)
❧	secrets	❧	cards and letters
❧	back rubs	❧	each other's friends
❧	shopping trips	❧	minutes, days, and hours
❧	desserts		
❧	long walks	❧	problems to be solved
❧	household hints	❧	heartaches
❧	ideas	❧	joys
❧	child care	❧	themselves

Something to ponder . . .

*This is something I love to share
with my friend . . .*

A Friendship Story

"Our family recently relocated to Pennsylvania from Arizona, and leaving my close friends was particularly difficult and painful. After our move, five of my dear girlfriends found a unique way to keep in touch and make me feel loved and missed. My husband had called these friends and asked them to plan a fortieth birthday/girlfriend bash for me because his gift to me was a trip to California and Arizona to celebrate with friends and family. . . .

"I was greeted at the airport by these normally attractive, well-dressed girlfriends in "*Old* Spice Girl" outfits. Their appearance was beyond description. Each outfit was complete with matching T-shirts with my picture, as a screaming two-year-old, on the front and the caption, 'Sherilyn is 40 but not a good sporty!' They had chosen personal "spice" names for each of us, neatly printed across our backs. My name was Paprika, but they referred to me as 'Reeka' and pronounced it only in a shrill scream.

"They whisked me away to a restroom in the airport and provided an outfit for me to change into. Soon I was adorned in skin-tight gold lamé bell-bottoms, four-inch white satin platform shoes with black tights, and a birthday T-shirt of my own. The outfit was complete with a sweet little tiara for my crown. They then paraded me all over town (movie, dinner, shopping mall) hootin' and hollerin' my spice name, my age, and many other birthday comments. We put big smiles on many faces!

"The remainder of the celebration included a two-night stay at a beautiful north Phoenix resort, a birthday cake, a manicure and pedicure, and hours of girl talk. It ended with another surprise party with many more friends, another costume (complete with a wig), a singing telegram by an old roommate, a skit, gifts, Mexican food (my favorite!) and more girl talk. It was a celebration like no other!

"Many of you may be thinking, 'If those are *friends*, I'd rather have enemies,' but you see, that's the glory of this tale; my friends knew that I would love such a celebration! I love people and I enjoy being crazy and having fun. That celebration was tailor-made for *me*; it was a labor of love. That is precisely what I cherish in these particular friendships."

—Sherilyn Jameson,
State College, Pennsylvania

Sharing the Load

Paintbrush in hand, Donna stood out in her yard next to her newly built, freshly stuccoed, unpainted fence and wondered if she would ever get it done in time.

Donna's husband, David, had built that fence himself over the past few weeks. Actually, it was more a wall than a fence, constructed of heavy concrete, and David had nearly crippled himself hauling and lifting the heavy blocks. Then the stucco man had come, and all that was left was to paint the fence. Donna really wanted to finish in time for David's birthday that night.

That's when the phone rang. It was Donna's friend Sue. "Whatcha doing?"

Donna told her. And ten minutes later Sue had arrived with paintbrush in hand, ready to work.

The fence was beautifully painted long before party time. David was thrilled with the finished fence. And Donna was warmed and encouraged by this reminder of what a privilege it is to share the workload of life with a generous, dedicated friend.

Sharing the load. That's just as vital a part of friendship as sharing the fun. And though it may be true that woman's work is never done, it's also true that we women have always been good at sweetening our tasks by helping each other when we can.

Working together, in fact, has always been an integral part of women's friendships.

Think of primitive women grinding corn side by side.

Think of pioneer women gathering for a quilting bee.

Think of your grandmother sitting on the porch with her friends and shelling peas or swapping stories over the back fence while the laundry flaps in the breeze.

And think of you and your friends doing whatever it is you do . . . together.

Maybe you're a quilter, too, and you love to gather at one friend's house to do your stitching.

Maybe you like to share mundane household chores—cleaning, cooking, laundry—with a friend. (We recommend it.)

Maybe you search for business projects or club work you can do as a team, or you turn your committee sessions into fun, but fruitful, social sessions.

If you're not in the habit of looking for ways to enjoy the company of friends while you work . . . well, then, that's something to explore. For there's something about working side by side that builds friendships like nothing else can. Working together not only lightens the burden; it also builds a shared history, and it helps you get to know each other better. In fact, there's no better way to learn a person's true character than to see her on the job.

When we were young wives and stay-at-home moms, we both learned the value of sharing housecleaning work with a friend. This, of course, was before we met, so we did this with other friends. We would get together at one house, clean house like mad, move over to another house and clean, then go get coffee together. Donna even made a pact with a special friend to clean together on Wednesdays while they prayed and fasted for their children. She and her friend maintained the pact for nearly three years. Their reward was a deeper sense of closeness to their children and to each other. As a bonus, the housework flew by twice as fast.

Of course, housecleaning is not the only kind of work that lends itself to cooperative arrangements. Almost any kind of chore—from painting the fence to stuffing envelopes to putting in a new drain—can be accomplished together. (We've never done plumbing together, but who's to say it can't be done?) And creative endeavors such as decorating a house or designing a publicity plan for the new museum show will almost always profit from the synergy of compatible minds.

And it's always possible, of course, for two friends to share a professional endeavor. We know a freelance writer who goes out of her way to procure assignments she can do with her best friend. The two of them live thousands of miles away from each other—in Minnesota and Texas—but they use the vehicle of shared work to give themselves more time together, sometimes with a tax write-off for phone calls!

As we see it, there are three basic ways that women can nurture friendships while working together, and we recommend seizing every opportunity.

First, you can get together to take care of tasks that are dull, repetitive, or just big and daunting. This can be anything from scrubbing floors to repainting walls to addressing Christmas cards to canning fruit. Teaming up to tackle your chores or projects together will almost always make the work fly by.

Second, you can use your creativity in searching out fun or challenging tasks for the two of you to do. Consider teaming up to direct a play, teach Sunday School, prepare a meal for the homeless, or take a college class. Whatever skills and concerns you share can become an opportunity for the two of you to grow closer and learn more about each other.

A third—and vital—way that friends can work together is to do what Donna's friend did: You can step into the breach and help when one person's workload turns into overload. Friends help friends, whether it's keeping the kids so she can make a work deadline, helping cook and clean when unexpected guests arrive, or answering the phone during an especially busy and stressful day.

Emilie still remembers the overwhelming gratitude she felt when she was in ill health and facing a huge holiday seminar . . . and Donna and David flew out at their own expense to help. For three days they carried boxes, stacked books, supervised volunteers, and ran interference for Emilie while she tried to keep her energy up. Donna's unquestioning willingness to step in and share the work was just about the best Christmas gift Emilie received that year.

However you decide to work together, with your friends, we believe you'll reap many of the same wonderful benefits we've discovered.

One, you get to enjoy one another's company—a great plus in itself.

Second, you'll probably feel less alone and less burdened. Just knowing that you have someone supporting you makes any workload a bit easier to bear.

Third, you get to know each other better than you ever could if all your interactions were merely social. You'll learn how your friend acts under pressure, how she approaches problems. And even if time pressures or difference in work styles lead to petty annoyances, you'll have the opportunity to work through these difficulties to a deeper level of understanding and trust. Working together gives you a chance to practice tolerance, patience, and forgiveness.

You're building your friendship . . . while you're getting things done.

Can you think of a more joyful or efficient way to work?

A Friendship Story

"Rose told me that she was pregnant. Less than two weeks later, I found out I was pregnant, too. It was so wonderful sharing such a blessed occasion with a good friend. When Rose would come over and need food *now* and then be picky about what I had to offer, I understood. We went through morning sickness together. We complained to each other when no one else wanted to hear it. (Yes, misery does love company!)

"Rose was due December 24; I was due January 7. We planned to watch each other's older kids(s) while we delivered the new one. . . . But God had a different plan.

"I got the flu and due to dehydration went into labor December 27. (Rose was still heavy with child.) . . . The first time they let me nurse Adam alone in my room . . . the nurse brought him to me and then returned almost immediately. She said, 'There's a woman walking through her labor out here and she wants to know if she can come in. She says her name is Rose.' . . .

"How sublime! . . . I had my precious gift from God at my breast and at the same time had the honor of experiencing labor with one of my best friends (she is also a gift from God). Several hours later I walked down to the labor and delivery area and . . . they let me go in. Jack was still 'wet behind the ears,' literally! They were weighing him and he was red and screaming. The bond I feel with both these little boys is amazing."

—Tammy Aragaki,
Phoenix, Arizona

Kindred in Spirit

We've been there so many times before —the two of us together somewhere, in Emilie's comfy garden room or Donna's welcoming den, or in a restaurant or an airport or a shopping mall, our heads together, our hearts joined, sharing a prayer or a word of hope before we continue with our day.

For as long as we've been friends, you see, we've been aware that the friendship we share is really a three-way relationship consisting of Emilie, Donna, and the God we both love.

That is not to say you can't be friends without sharing a faith. It happens all the time. People without any kind of spiritual orientation manage to nurture powerful bonds of caring. People with different religious beliefs manage to transcend their differences and enjoy fruitful friendships. We've seen it. We've done it, for we, too, have friends whom we cherish but who do not share our faith.

And yet . . .

And yet we've found that the spiritual commonality that undergirds our particular friendship does give it a kind of strength and sweetness we don't experience in those other friendships. The bond of our shared spiritual commitment connects us at a much deeper, more powerful level than the simple bonds of human attraction and affection.

We love the picture painted in the Book of Ecclesiastes: "A threefold cord is not quickly broken" (4:12). To us, that is a picture of the two of us entwined in a friendship that includes God as a third member. It's like silken cords girded with steel. We trust it. We cherish it.

Not that we always agree with each other regarding every belief, every interpretation. We don't. But we do share an orientation of belief and a devotion that is a fundamental part of who we are. We are both Christians. Our Christian faith is vital to both of us. And we find that our faith is a common thread that holds us together when things are difficult, that gives us strength in our togetherness, that makes this friendship more than an association of two people who do similar work and enjoy similar activities.

From the very first, there has been a sense of sacredness in what we share together—not just the prayers and the Bible study and the spiritual talk, but everything we do.

And we certainly don't spend all our time together with hands folded and heads bowed!

But that's exactly beside the point . . . which is that our relationship with the One who made us and saves us and sustains us is woven into all aspects of our relationship with each other. It is a part of us—a deep, harmonious chord that grounds the dancing music of our time together.

Yes, we do pray together and for each other. We rest secure in the knowledge that we are in each other's prayers.

Yes, we do talk about what we believe and what we have experienced as people of faith. We share the thoughts we've gleaned from reading Scripture and the insights we believe the Holy Spirit has given us.

Yes, we love to worship together when it is possible, to share the experience of praising our God.

But we also laugh together—sometimes until our stomachs hurt—over something we've heard or something we've remembered. And that laughter, too, is part of our shared faith. To us it is holy laughter.

We support each other, and that sense of support is buoyed by knowing we are both loved of God. We try to care for each other both emotionally and physically, even as we trust God to take care of us both. And to us that mutual care is a holy thing as well.

We go shopping together and visit with other friends, and even as we compare prices and serve tea, the commonality of our spirits informs our choices and our attitudes.

Quite simply, the way we *are* is born out of where we put our trust, and where we put our trust is the essence of our life together as friends.

In our experience, at least, kindred spirits draw even closer when they share a kindred faith.

A Circle of Love

When you marry, you marry more than a person. You also marry into a family and into a set of friends and acquaintances. Your circle of love intersects with his circle of love—and his people, in a sense, will become your people.

We believe that's true of friendships as well.

Although it's possible to maintain a friendship that is more or less separate from other connections, we don't believe it's usual or even desirable. It's certainly not easy. For no woman, to paraphrase John Donne, is an island. Every one of us exists in a network of connections: mother, father, sisters, brothers, spouse, and friends. And it's almost impossible to nurture a deep connection to another person without being connected to her network as well.

Most of the time, this is a joy.

Sometimes it's a bit of a struggle, for loving a friend doesn't guarantee you'll automatically enjoy spending time with her family or other friends.

But the kind of deep, enduring friendships we've come to appreciate the most are the ones in which we can open our arms to embrace each other's children, grandchildren, husbands, significant others, and friends.

One thing we've really appreciated about our friendship is that our men are involved in it as well. From the beginning, we've liked the fact that Bob and David approve of our friendship—they like us to be together. Now we enjoy being "couple friends," and the time we spend together as a foursome is usually fun and fulfilling. We also like the fact that our husbands enjoy each other's company. That frees us to spend more time doing "girl things" together.

We also love feeling like second parents to each other's children. Emilie's children and grandchildren are folded into

Donna's heart. Donna's daughter is like Emilie's own child. And this is a wonderful gift, especially in those times when we cannot seem to talk to our own children. We cherish having someone who loves them almost as much as we do, who will care for them and guide them and speak the truth to them in love when we cannot speak it or they cannot hear it from our own lips. And we didn't really do it on purpose, but now we can see that our children have learned about friendship by watching us. Emilie's daughter Jenny told Donna recently, "I love watching you and my mom be friends!"

As for the friends of our friends . . . we have had such fun meeting and spending time with the people in each other's lives. After all, if they have something in common with our friend, they're likely to have something in common with us as well!

That doesn't mean that we have all become the closest of friends. Emilie has some dear friends that Donna just hasn't bonded with, and vice versa. We know other women friends whose husbands don't get along that well or whose children resist friendly overtures or whose close friends just can't see what they see in other friends.

We don't think that has to be a problem, necessarily. Friends don't have to share everything in common . . . even the people they love.

But even when we can't share affection, we can honor our friends' friends and family.

Usually it's enough to respect their commitments and not make our friends feel torn between us and the other people they love. Usually it's enough to be cordial and gracious when we meet the others in our friends' lives and to show them caring and compassion for friendship's sake.

Even in those rare cases when we feel another friend or a family member poses a danger, we are wise to choose our words carefully, weighing our honest concerns with our understanding.

But the good news is that, most of the time, this is simply not a problem.

Most of the time a friend of a friend becomes, if not a cherished companion, then at least a friendly acquaintance.

Most of the time the family of your friend becomes, if not your own extended family, at least a group of people you can love for her sake.

Most of the time, when our circles of love intersect, there's simply more love to go around.

And in this world where so many people feel friendless and uncared-for, more love can't help but be a good thing.

A Friendship Story

"A group of 25 girls began a club in 1929 which has lasted to 1999 and beyond. There are 17 women left in this group and the Lord has had His hand on each of our lives. There was a prayer we would all say together at our meetings. We have shared our lives about dates, engagements, weddings, baby showers, and now the third generation are sometimes at our gatherings. Our husbands have been associated with our group for many years so we wouldn't be driving long distances alone. Philanthropic work was done in the earlier years and our mothers were honored each year. Many in the group have traveled extensively and we have all benefited from this. The original group did not smoke or drink and there were no divorces in the group. Many women have lost their husbands, two doctors and a judge among them. Eight couples in the group have had 50 or more years together. It has been an unusual friendship over these many years."

—Roie Alys Underhill,
Hemet, California

33 Fun and Fruitful Ideas for Being Together

1. Read a book aloud—or start a "circle of friends" book club.
2. Do all your cooking for a week in double batches, then freeze them.
3. Pack a lunch in backpacks and take a *long* walk.
4. Make an appointment for two at a day spa. Get facials, massage, manicures—whatever makes you feel most pampered and beautiful.
5. Spend an autumn afternoon planting bulbs together.
6. Learn to make stained glass.
7. Pray together.
8. Expand your understanding by attending a service of a different denomination or faith.
9. Team up on big chores like organizing the pantry or painting the bedrooms.
10. Drive to a nearby small town and have lunch in a little place where you've never been before.
11. Meet in another city for a weekend.
12. Rent a movie and gather both families together to watch it.
13. Celebrate a holiday together.
14. Sing or play a duet on piano, guitar, or kazoo.
15. Work together on a service project: serving at a soup line, repairing houses for the elderly, reading stories to children.
16. Cook a meal for a shut-in friend and deliver it together.
17. Team-teach a class at your local hobby store, university extension, or neighborhood center.
18. Cross-stitch matching pillows for your sofas.

19. Schedule a "put in album" day for all those photos that have piled up.

20. On *another* day, spend the afternoon thumbing through albums and looking at photos of each other from grade school, high school, and college. You may laugh, but kindly!

21. Rent or borrow a video camera if you don't own one and shoot videos of each other's families.

22. Have a "friends of friends" party. Ask each guest to bring a guest the others probably don't know. Have fun meeting people from many different walks of life and actively expand your circles of love.

23. Spend your lunch hour at the skating rink.

24. Buy or make kites and take them to the park to fly. (If the kids are good, they can come along.)

25. Set up two ironing boards, pop a great CD in the player, and take care of all your "pressing" concerns.

26. Get tough. Go shopping!

27. Make a date to attend the "twilight" matinee— usually the least expensive showing, around 4:30 P.M.—of the newest "chick flick" in town. Bring lots of tissues.

28. Have breakfast together early on a Friday or Saturday and then go garage-sale hopping. Bring a newspaper, a local map, and some cash (many sales don't take checks).

29. Play a game of Monopoly or Scrabble.

30. Plan a party for your other friends.

31. Refinish old furniture together.

32. Give each other a back rub or a foot rub . . . or both!

33. Write a book together!

Just Being

Just recently we spent the weekend together at Emilie's house. And it was wonderful!

We didn't work.

We didn't go out to shop or see a movie.

We didn't get together with other friends.

Sometimes we didn't even talk.

We simply enjoyed being with each other.

We read a little.

We took a nap.

We reminisced quietly.

We prayed.

What a sweet, precious time of being together, rejoicing in the warmth and security of knowing you're with someone who loves to be with you.

That's something to remember always, when you're spending time with a friend of the heart.

Play together.

Work together.

Share your spirits.

Share the people in your life.

But make sure there's some time left over just to be . . . together.

Something to ponder . . .

*Here's something I want to do with
my friend this week . . .*

The ABC's of Friendship

We didn't invent this one, but we love it!

A Friend . . .

Accepts you as you are.
Believes in you.
Calls you just to say "hi."
Doesn't give up on you.
Envisions the whole of you, even the unfinished parts.
Forgives your mistakes.
Gives unconditionally.
Helps you.
Invites you over to
Just "be" with you.
Keeps you close at heart.
Loves you for who you are.
Makes a difference in your life.
Never judges.
Offers support.
Picks you up.
Quiets your fears.
Raises your spirits.
Says nice things about you.
Tells you the truth when you need to hear it.
Understands you.
Values you.
Walks beside you.
X-plains things you don't understand.
Yells when you won't listen and
Zaps you back to reality!

—Author unknown

"Friendship," said
Christopher Robin,
"is a very comforting
sort of thing to have."

—A. A. MILNE

4

"You Make Me Feel Loved"

The Care and Maintenance of Treasured Friends

Whatever you yourself desire, I will do it for you.

—The Book of First Samuel

Like a Garden

We're not the first people to observe that friendship is like a garden. But we love to think of it that way, because we like to think of our relationships as lovely, leafy, growing, life-giving.

And, of course, that reminds us that friendships, like gardens, need care.

Yes, you can plant a seed and let it take care of itself, and something probably will grow.

But you get the best results with a lot of watering and fertilizing and weeding and nurturing.

Besides, caring for each other is one of the basic purposes of friendship. We all need the encouragement, the understanding, the advocacy that a friendship brings us. We all need the reassurance that we are worth some trouble.

And here's something else: In a sense, it's the very act of caring for our friendships that make them so precious to us. We tend to love those things in which we've invested our time, our energies, our money, our efforts. As the poet Ezra Pound put it, "What thou lov'st well is thy true heritage."

That's one reason we love our well-tended gardens—not just for the fruits and the flowers, but also for the pruning, the spraying, the pulling, for the investments of seed and fertilizer, even for the sunburn and the blisters.

We love best those things (and those people) in which we have invested acts of love.

Even better, we love those things (and those people) in which the investment of love is a mutual thing.

Two gardens can't care for each other.

But two people can.

And that, to an important degree, is what friends are for.

Everyday Maintenance

*H*ow do you take care of a friendship? A lot of it just comes naturally. As you spend time together and enjoy each other and help each other, chances are you're also taking care of each other and nurturing your friendship. And yet, like any other worthwhile relationships, friendship blossoms most beautifully with the investment of a little deliberate care and nurturing.

Most of the time, a little everyday maintenance is all you need to keep a friendship growing. A phone call. An e-mail. A quick note scrawled at the bottom of a funny card and dropped in the mailbox. A touch on the arm or a hug in passing. A quick visit and a chat and a promise to get together again soon. A thoughtful gift. A silly surprise.

Years ago, when Donna had decided to whip her nonathletic body in shape and had finally dared her first 10K race, a good friend met her at the finish line and plopped a laurel wreath on her panting, perspiring head.

More recently, Emilie's good friend Barbara surprised her with the gift of antique tea towels inscribed with "sister." (Then Emilie had a set embroidered for Donna!)

All of our friends love to send cards back and forth, to scribble notes on the backs of photographs and pop them in envelopes. We love to collect little remembrances from antique shops or even toy stores and give them to our friends, or to cook up special recipes of goodies to share. We love to pick up the phone and share a cup of tea together while we chat.

And it is these little gifts and gestures between friends that help keep us connected, that comfort and encourage us, that remind us of how much we care and are cared for.

Faithfulness in little things helps, too. You are caring for your friendship when you show up for your coffee date, when you think twice about canceling your walk together, when you make a note to pray for your friend—then read the note and actually do it. Kept promises fertilize a friendship.

And just as weeding is part of caring for a garden, addressing the problems between you is a vital part of everyday friendship maintenance. In even the best friendships you will encounter petty annoyances, minor hurts, feelings of neglect and distance.

Your friend is too busy one week to call you.

Or you show up consistently late for your lunch dates.

Or one of you suspects the other of breaking a confidence.

Or you simply exchange sharp words on a bad day.

Like weeds, negative feelings between friends can grow if left untended. They have even been known to choke a friendship. So the thing to do when problems occur is to take care of them while they are fresh and small.

And notice: Taking care of problems does not always require a confrontation. It doesn't always even call for a conversation. Sometimes you will simply choose to recognize and dismiss the problem. You will say to yourself, "Oh, she's just stressed out," or "She's just too snowed-under to call," or "That's just the way she is."

And then you realize that you really do trust your friend's love. You understand why the problem happened. You *love* her just the way she is. You're willing to let the matter slide, to put the hurt behind you.

That really is a valid way to handle some problems between friends.

But be careful. Because letting a matter slide can also be a way to avoid resolving issues. And when you fail to resolve real issues, you allow a distance to grow between you.

Unresolved anger, feelings of betrayal, feelings of hurt—these can easily choke out a friendship.

When in doubt, then, it's better to talk. Sometimes nurturing a friendship means gently confronting your friend. It means confessing your feelings of hurt or anger. It means swallowing your pride and apologizing . . . or opening your heart to forgive. It means saying again these words: "You matter to me. I don't want to hurt you. You are worth so much more to me than my hurt feelings and my pride."

Taking care of problems—that's just a part of everyday business in any relationship, friendships included. And it's better done sooner than later.

Most of all, everyday maintenance is a matter of keeping each other in mind, even when you can't get together.

It means remembering why a particular day is special . . . or hard . . . and making a point to find out how it went.

It means knowing what is going on with each other's family and work, and keeping up with what's new.

It means checking in on a regular basis, just to know that everything's going all right.

It means doing what you can, when you can, to make your friend feel loved.

These are the everyday connections that nurture friendship. They are the little reminders that say: "Yes, I'm still here. I know you're there, too. Never, ever forget that I care about you."

That kind of everyday maintenance doesn't actually have to take place every day. How often you touch base will depend a lot on where you live, what you do, what your expectations for each other are.

And it doesn't really involve much time or energy or money—but it requires some. It's just a matter of paying attention, of giving your friendship some priority, of reminding yourself that friendship is not a luxury and that friendships can't thrive without a little attention. When you are parceling out the pieces of yourself, it's important to reserve a chunk for the friends of your heart.

For ordinary, everyday care of a relationship, think *little things—regularly and often.*

Think contact and constancy, watering and weeding.

Then think . . . daisies and gardenias, avocados and artichokes—a flowering, fragrant garden of love and delight.

A well-nourished, well-cultivated friendship of the heart.

Extravagance

Not all gestures of friendship are little, of course.

Friends of the heart not only love daily and faithfully; they also know how to love extravagantly when extravagance is appropriate.

When your friend is in need, it's appropriate to do everything you can to *be* there, to help. Even if it means taking a day off work. Even if it means giving up your weekends or driving hundreds of miles. Even (and this is hard!) if it means giving up her attention so that she can get some much needed rest. . . .

When your friend celebrates a milestone—a wedding, a graduation, the opening of a new business, or the start of a new phase in life—it's appropriate to splurge on something very special. Even if it means organizing an extravagant reunion. Even if it means traveling out of town and shopping for hours to find just the perfect gift. Even if it means months and months of needlework to finish a handmade gift or hours and hours at the computer putting together just the perfect written tribute.

When you have been friends for a while and you want to express just how much she means to you, it's appropriate to pull out all the stops (in terms of finance or of time or of effort) to give her just the perfect gift or find the perfect words to say what you really feel. Even if it means spending a little more than you can afford or going to more shops than you have time to visit or planning far in advance or staying up half the night.

You see, thrift is a good thing.

Prudence is a good thing.

Wisdom is definitely a good thing. And it's wise to count the cost of relationship, to set your boundaries in terms of how much time and effort and money you can afford to invest in any given relationship.

But when it comes to friends of your heart, it's also a good thing sometimes to throw caution to the wind and give beyond what is thrifty. Beyond what is prudent. Beyond what some people might think is wise.

Thus, we know women who have given away a cherished family heirloom to a treasured friend: their mother's ring, a beloved painting or book, a carefully guarded piece of antique porcelain. Donna's friend Anne Johnson once made Donna cry over the gift of her grandmother's special cranberry dish—and the thought of that loving gift can still bring tears to Donna's eyes.

We know women who have flown cross-country to support a friend during a time of family crisis and have stayed for weeks, helping with the driving and the laundry and the meals, helping their friends go on when the way was difficult.

We know women who have listened for hours while their bereaved friends talked through their grief again and again . . . or have given up weekends to baby-sit . . . or have offered their sofas and their extra rooms for days or weeks or months . . . or have helped nurse their friend's elderly parents . . . or have even walked with friends into the valley of the shadow of death.

Jesus of Nazareth once said, "Greater love has no one than this, than to lay down one's life for his friends." But laying down one's life for someone doesn't necessarily mean literally dying for them. What it does mean is willing and joyful sacrifice—of your time, of your freedom, of your ease, of your financial resources and your prized possessions. It means the generous, unthrifty, imprudent giving of yourself to someone you love. To your friend.

Now, you wouldn't do it for everyone.

You wouldn't do it all of the time for anyone.

But for your special, well-loved friend of the heart, an act of sacrifice can be a lovely and beautiful gesture. It can bring surprising joy to both giver and recipient. It can bring the two of you closer than you've ever been.

And yes, there are pitfalls to beware when it comes to extravagant giving. The giver must watch her motives, being sure that her giving is not a form of manipulation, a guilt-lever or bribe. It must not be an attempt to win friendship or to shore up one's own feelings of insecurity. It must not feel like charity or one-upmanship.

Even an extravagant, sacrificial gift, in other words, must be just that—a gift. The only strings attached must be heartstrings.

For the recipient, the primary pitfall is pride and discomfort. It can feel strange to be the recipient of generous, heartfelt, over-the-top giving. The challenge is to accept the sacrifice with gratitude and humility, to return the love without feeling the need to top the gift.

And all this means that prudence and wisdom do enter into the situation after all.

It really is important to count the cost of going all out, to weigh the risks and ponder the consequences.

But just as important sometimes is to decide a friend is worth whatever it takes.

And it's true.

A true friend of the heart is worth almost anything you choose to give.

A Double Friendship Story

"I met my friend Marina Papineau through my daughter's friendship with her son. Our children were 'sweethearts' at the time of their eighth grade graduation in 1995. It was at that reception that Marina asked me, 'Will we still be friends if our kids break up?' My response was, 'I'm not your friend because of our children. . . . Our friendship's foundation is strong and the only thing that will change is for our friendship to become stronger.'

"Marina and I have been friends now for more than five years. Whenever we are together it's as though we are schoolgirls. We both love 'tea time,' and that is what really made our friendship. We try new tearooms on occasion, or one will invite the other into our home for that 'special' time together. I call Marina my 'teapot' friend, because she *always* knows when my cup needs to be filled with that refreshing flavor of love. . . .

"We have regular activities we do together annually. At Christmas we attend a different activity each year: a ballet, symphony, children's choir, craft fairs at each season, but our favorite spot several times a year is having lunch at Hellos, our favorite tearoom. I look forward to the years in which we grow old 'gracefully' together. And I'm very certain this friendship will last for eternity, because our heavenly Father is preparing a 'tearoom' for us."

—Dawn Beaty,
Westfield, Indiana

"It is hard to say the precise moment my friendship started with my close friend, Dawn Beaty. My son and her daughter had started liking each other in junior high. (They are both seniors now.) We knew who each other was as we lived just down the street from each other. Somehow, we both decided to take our daughters to our favorite tea room, Hellos, before school started. We so enjoyed the day that this has become a yearly outing with our daughters. . . .

"I always look forward to our outings. The time we spend together just flies by. There are times where I feel like I have neglected her with my hectic schedule. I just call Dawn and say we must get together, I need my cup filled with her love and friendship. We do so much together. We have been to several tearooms, the ballet, the symphony, shopping at craft fairs, our children's sporting events, and for the first time a weekend trip to a bed and breakfast. Each Christmas we take a day for ourselves and plan something we have not done before. It is so exciting to plan our outing and then to just relax and enjoy it. . . .

"I know that she has filled my cup to overflowing so many times. It could just be a card, a wave as she drives by, or just five minutes on the phone and I feel my heart bursting. I can always walk away and know that I am smiling all the way home. She is always there willing to listen and help out. . . . As I talk to the Lord, I always make sure I tell Him thank you for sending her to me. He knows how much I need her."

—Marina Papineau,
Westfield, Indiana

In Short: A Summary of Friendship Maintenance

It's the little, thoughtful touches that keep your garden growing.

It's the big, extravagant, over-the-top gestures that twine your hearts together forever.

Think: A daisy a day . . . and sometimes a roomful of roses.

Something to ponder. . .

If I could give my friend anything in the world, it would be . . .

A Friendship Story

"I met a lovely lady, Helen Quinn, and we became friends immediately. We lived 35 miles apart, so we made an effort to see each other. She was one of the busiest, most productive people I ever met.

"I probably knew her six months before she told me she had had a radical mastectomy many years before. A year or so later I was diagnosed with breast cancer and had to have a modified radical mastectomy.

"God is good. He put Helen in my life not only to be a wonderful friend, but to be strength at a time of crisis in my life. She was my living proof there is life (abundant life) after a mastectomy.

"My surgery was 25 years ago. Hers was 40 years ago. We are still wonderful friends."

—Dianne Mills,
Riverside, California

Touch Me

Don't you love to watch tiny little girls playing together?

They run and jump and turn somersaults. They hug and give each other slobbery kisses. And when they walk together, they hold hands.

And so do grown-up girls sometimes. Even gray-haired girls.

Several years ago we were together in Oregon for a series of meetings. We stayed in the same hotel, and one afternoon we decided to take a walk together near the hotel.

What a lovely place to walk! The trees were green. The flowers were bright and cheerful. The breeze was fresh and soft. We rejoiced in the fun of being there, the sheer joy of being together.

So we walked and we talked and we laughed and we prayed. And soon we were walking hand in hand.

The funny thing is, we didn't even realize it until we noticed that other people were looking at us a little strangely. Startled, we let our hands drop. *What are they thinking?* And then we thought, *Who cares?* We linked hands again and walked on in trust and love like the two little playmates that we still are.

For more and more, as we've grown together as friends, we've also grown to understand the connective power of touch in friendship.

Yes, friends touch hearts, but sometimes the way to the heart is through the skin.

That could mean holding hands or linking arms while you walk or pray. It could mean a warm hug or just a tender touch on the shoulder. It could be as simple as giving one another a facial or fixing each other's hair. It can be as playful as propping your legs up together on a table or sitting back-to-back on a sun-warmed rock at the beach.

When you do that, of course, the connection is more than skin-deep. Touching links people at far deeper levels than just talking or being together could ever do. When you touch your friend, you convey warmth and comfort. You communicate trust and acceptance. You share your energy. You speak your love in a language far deeper than words.

This, we have found, is especially vital during times of stress or illness. When we feel vulnerable and our strength is depleted, we crave the nondemanding, energy-giving quality of a friend's touch.

Emilie learned that anew in the months when chemo-therapy had worn her down and left her weak. During those times, she found herself craving the touch of others. A hug from a friend felt like a lifeline, the touch of a hand like an infusion of strength. Even on days when she just didn't feel like talking, she felt like being held.

No wonder that those who work with the dying in hospice organizations are trained to crawl right up in bed with the patients and hold them. Touch communicates life, even to the dying. It communicates love and warmth.

Different friendships, or course, will involve different levels of physical touch. People differ in the amount of touch they're comfortable with in a friendship, and part of loving a friend involves respecting her physical boundaries. And it is certainly possible to maintain a close, loving friendship with a minimum of touch, especially among people who were raised to express their caring in less tactile ways.

And yet we've found that as any friendship grows, as trust grows, the level of touch almost always grows with it. And even a polite "good-bye" hug becomes capable of expressing so much of the love and trust the heart holds.

And we—well, we don't even worry about it anymore. Touching each other is simply part of who we are together.

We are happy to embrace, happy to offer shoulder rubs, happy to link arms. When we get together, you might even find us walking, holding hands.

Just two little girls together.

The Gift of a Friend

To my friend . . .

> You give me the freeing gift of your acceptance
> The strengthening gift of your trust.
> The comforting gift of your acceptance
> The relaxing gift of our commonality.
> Your honest words give me the courageous gift
>   of truth
> And when you forgive me—as often you do,
>   my whole heart is gifted with grace.
> The gift of your laughter lightens my load.
> The gift of your tears washes my spirit clean.
> Sweet friend,
> Your very life is a gift to me.

Something to ponder . . .

These are the special gifts my
friend has given me . . .

46 Great Gifts to Give a Friend (Besides Yourself!)

1. A phone call—with a follow-up to ask, "How did it go?"
2. Your daily prayers.
3. A photo of the two of you in a beautiful frame, or a collection of photos in a "multiple" frame.
4. A book from your personal library with your notes in the margins.
5. A family memento, with a note explaining it.
6. A thrift-shop treasure: a miniature pitcher, a demitasse spoon, a crocheted dresser scarf.
7. Something for her collection, or something to start a new one.
8. Personalized stationery you made yourself.
9. Something that made you laugh when you saw it in the store or catalog.
10. A basket of small items chosen around a given theme: tea, roses, the ocean.
11. Supplies for a hobby she wants to try.
12. A mug, a tea bag, and a phone card with a note saying, "Let's have tea together over the phone."
13. Something she just loved but reluctantly put down when you were shopping together.
14. A replacement for a treasured item she's lost.
15. A monogrammed Bible, hymnal, or prayer book.
16. A packet of assorted greeting cards that she can send, plus a beautiful pen.
17. A video of one of her favorite movies.
18. A CD or cassette of her favorite musical artist.
19. An inspirational tape of one of your pastor's favorite sermons.
20. A handmade gift you and the children made during the holiday season.

21. A camping trip together.
22. A chain of encouraging cards and notes when she is going through a difficult time.
23. A personalized scrapbook of pictures and memorabilia from your times together.
24. A personalized calendar featuring pictures of you, her, and your families (make on computer or have made at a copy store).
25. A hand-painted T-shirt to match yours!
26. A manicure, pedicure, or massage.
27. A surprise visit (when you live out of town).
28. Free baby-sitting (offer to let all the kids stay with you overnight!).
29. Dinner for her family.
30. A joke or a cartoon.
31. A craft kit or a lesson.
32. Movie tickets.
33. An oil change or fill-up at the gas station.
34. A cookie bouquet: Bake flower shapes on wooden dowels, ice with bright colors, and arrange in a basket with florist's foam.
35. Help with a project.
36. A single gourmet chocolate.
37. Bath salts or scented oils.
38. Fancy paper clips (Donna's favorite!).
39. A bag of jelly beans.
40. A candle with a luscious scent.
41. Coupons or gift certificates.
42. An adorable stuffed toy or doll.
43. A lush green plant or a big bouquet of flowers.
44. A carefully chosen memento from your travels (we like shopping antique shops for special souvenirs).
45. A hand-chosen bookmark.
46. A custom Christmas ornament.

Friendship Makers, Friendship Breakers

With every good gift there comes a temptation.

With every good thing comes the possibility of misuse.

And this is true, unfortunately, of the good gift of friendship.

Because friends are human, and because humans are flawed and sometimes immature or selfish, any intimate relationship carries with it the risk of hurting or being hurt.

Don't get us wrong! Friendship is worth the risk.

But it's also a good idea to think ahead about the attitudes that can make or break a friendship—and how damage can be healed or prevented.

Jealousy and possessiveness, for example, can stunt the growth of a healthy friendship. These attitudes usually crop up as a result of immaturity and insecurity and the natural human tendency to keep good things for ourselves. We may not be quite as obvious about it as children are: "She's *my* friend." But that's the way we feel sometimes. We find ourselves comparing the time our friend spends with us against the time she spends with her family, her job, her other friends. Or we may encounter pressure from one friend to drop another friend. We may find ourselves uncomfortable when we realize that more than one person considers us her *very best* friend!

But there's a reason that *friendship* and *freedom* start with the same letter! Healthy friendship thrives on freedom. A true friend encourages and supports her friend's relationships because she knows that one person can't belong to another and that it's impossible for one person to completely fill another's needs. Besides, friendship cannot be bought or demanded or controlled, no matter how insecure we feel.

Jealousy and possessiveness are far more likely to drive friends away than to keep them close.

Dishonesty can harm friendships in a number of ways. It can lead to mistrust and a sense of betrayal—when a friend discovers that her friend hasn't been honest with her. Or it can lead to distance and alienation—because one person is hiding what she really thinks and who she really is. Friendships need the light of truth the way a garden needs the sunlight. There can be no real sense of trust and intimacy without the secure knowledge that your friend will tell you the truth, even when it's hard.

On the other hand, the *lack of restraint and respect* in friendship—even under the auspices of telling the truth—can easily shrivel tender leaves of friendship. This is a commonly misunderstood reality in our "let it all hang out" society. Yes, friendships thrive on honesty and openness. But this doesn't mean saying everything you think, all the time! Even with the closest friend, there is a time to hold back, to soften your comments, to defer the gratification of "coming clean" for the sake of your friend's feelings or her happiness. And there is a place for privacy even among intimate friends. The boundaries for each friendship may be different. But a friend of the heart will respect both her friend's boundaries and her own.

A friend will also keep her word, because *betrayed confidences and broken promises* are especially deadly to friendship. In fact, nothing will kill a friendship faster than a string of betrayals, small or large.

And *laziness* hurts a friendship like stingy watering hurts a garden—it can lead to withering or even a long, slow, painful death. The trouble is, it's easy to become lazy with a close friend you take for granted. It's easy to overlook birthdays, to forget to call, to neglect coming over because you know your friend will always be there. The problem is, maybe she won't!

Is competition a problem in friendship? Not necessarily! Friends sharpen friends, and there really is such a thing as healthy competition even among friends of the heart. The real problem, as we see it, is insecurity and envy. Healthy competition can sharpen you, but envy is a sure killer of relationships. It's hard to love someone when you desperately want what she has.

Perhaps the most deadly of the common friendship breakers is *pride*. And the reason pride is so dangerous is that it gets in the way of the healing process. When there has been a rift in a relationship, the only road to healing leads through apology and forgiveness. And often it is pride and stubbornness that make an apology so difficult, a forgiving word so hard to utter. So pride can prevent the reconciliation of loving friends.

Friendship breakers—that's an appropriate name for these all-too-common, all-too-harmful things that friends do and friends feel. Unfortunately, they can happen to any of us, and any of us can be guilty.

But here's the good news: There's really no need to dwell on friendship breakers because they all can be overcome by the friendship makers.

To us, it makes more sense to cultivate these positive traits and attitudes than to worry too much about negative ones.

And what are the friendship makers? They are the qualities that enable you to care for the garden of your friendship and to get past the damage caused by possessiveness or dishonesty or lack of restraint or broken promises.

What qualities of the heart will keep the gardens of your friendship growing vigorously? These are qualities that are worth cultivating right alongside your most precious relationships. Not only will they bring you better friendships; they'll also make you a better person. Here are some of them:

You need a generous heart to counteract the natural human tendency to grab and grasp. The more you practice opening your heart and your hands, the more you will know the freedom that comes with having a true friend of the heart—a friend whose love and devotion you really trust.

You need an open and honest heart to build trust with the truth.

You need a patient heart to grow friendship slowly, on good solid ground.

You need a discerning heart and disciplined tongue to balance honesty with kindness and discretion. A faithful heart will give you the strength you need to keep your promises.

You need a devoted heart to help you put your friend's best interests first and to do hard things for the sake of a friendship—whether that means confronting a friend or just accepting her as she is.

Most of all, you need *a forgiving, accepting heart* to enable you to move past the inevitable hurt in a friendship. Without forgiveness, how could any of us remain in a relationship?

An intimate, ongoing friendship, you see, must be made up of equal parts of truth and grace. There are times to confront, times to let a problem go.

There are times to drift, times to pull tightly together.

And always there is a risk, a possibility that the garden of a friendship could wither or fade.

The risk is worth it, but you should count the cost.

It takes a lot of heart to keep a friendship lush and green.

A Friendship Story

"I have some very special friends. I would call them my heart friends. They are friends who have seen me through the worst and the best. They have put up with me.

"One friend—Freddie—. . . always has to listen to my story in a round-about way before I get to the end, but she loves me unconditionally. We have been through the fire together.

"Rhonda and Lisa—they led me through some places in my heart I never knew were there. They met me and just accepted me and let me into their lives. . . .

"Then there's Susan. When I moved in next door to this girl, she came over and visited and visited. . . . I think back and know that I didn't treat her too wonderfully. I missed home and this was a new place and I wanted to go back. Thank God, we can't go back. Susan became a friend like no other . . . because of what she did. She prayed for the two friends I just mentioned. She knew what I needed and she prayed them in. She prayed for me daily, yet I never knew. She loved me so unconditionally that she had to let me go. Yet what a beautiful blessing—God has brought us back together with more love and understanding than ever before."

—Pamela Davis,
Seymour, Texas

What Do You Expect?

Unhealthy expectations for a friend

See me every day
Call me every week
Invite me to every party
Do everything with me
Do things the way I think they should be done
Don't ever hurt me
Be perfect

Healthy expectations for a friend

Do what you say you'll do
Show me respect
Value my growth
Value my family and friends (even if they're not yours)
Respect my faith
Keep your promises to me
Don't do anything knowingly that would hurt me
Talk to me about what your expectations are

Something to ponder . . .

These are my bottom-line expectations
for a friendship . . .

12 Wonderful Ways to Nurture Your Friendship

1. Make time to talk and listen on a regular basis.
2. Make your friend's spiritual well-being a priority. Pray for her always.
3. Give your friend her freedom. Let her be who she is without trying to change her. Give her freedom to be different from you.
4. Give her the gift of your discretion. Even with a close friend, some things may not need to be said. Others need to be said very carefully and gently.
5. Tell your friend what you like about her. Offer verbal encouragement.
6. Confront her when necessary, but in a spirit of love.
7. Respect her other relationships (even those people you don't especially like).
8. Make sure you have fun together. If you have to, make dates to go out and play.
9. Say thank you again and again.
10. Try to touch base even during busy times. Even a one-minute phone call is enough to sing a song, read a short inspirational thought, or just say good morning.
11. Forgive and forgive and forgive. Ask forgiveness when you even suspect you might need it.
12. Treasure your shared past. Remind each other of your favorite memories.

❧ ❧ ❧

"Make new friends,
but keep the old.
One is silver and
the other gold."

—CAMP SONG

❧ ❧ ❧

5

"It Seems Like We've Always Been Friends"

The Seasons of a Lasting Friendship

A friend loves at all times.

—THE BOOK OF PROVERBS

Annuals and Perennials

If friendship is a garden, then some friendships are annuals.

They bloom for a season, bringing joy, coloring our days. But then, when their season is gone, they wither and fade and they are gone from our lives, if not from our memories.

And this is as it should be. Not all friendships were made to last forever.

But some friendships do last—blooming season after season, year after year. They are our perennial friendships—the faithful, dependable blooms that return to our lives again and again.

They may lie dormant for one season or another, only to spring to life again. Or they may live on quietly, persistently fresh, like fragrant evergreens.

And oh, what a beauty these evergreen friends bring to the garden of our friendship. They are ones, most often, that become the beloved friends of the heart.

How wonderful to know, in a world that so often betrays us, that we can depend on the love and the care of our perennial friends.

But here's something to remember always as we tend the garden that is our lives: Perennials need care, too. They require the careful, faithful tending that recognizes they are a true investment. The way you water these special relationships, the fertilizer you give them—all these things will shape your garden for seasons to come.

What is the best way to tend these long-seasoned beauties?

First, give them honor. Express your appreciation and your love with words and with thoughtful gestures.

Second, pay them special attention. It's human nature to take the faithful and the familiar for granted. Resist the temptation! These are the friendships you need to give first choice on your appointment calendar—cancel other activities, if necessary, if these friends are in need.

Third, trust their rhythms. Allow them to ebb and flow. This may sound contradictory. How do you pay attention to a long-term friendship and still let it wax and wane? Well, that comes with trust and understanding. A well-established friendship can be trusted to survive dormant periods. A friend who is with you for the long haul can understand that there will be times when you barely have time or energy to touch base. It can survive times when you don't see each other every day or don't call each other every week. So although you should give your friendship honor and as much attention as you can, you don't need to worry too much if you or your friend are less available at certain times. Talk about it . . . then move forward in trust and understanding.

Here's a fourth way to nurture your long-standing friendship: Tell its story. Shared memories are the roots that keep your perennial friendships fresh and green. You don't need to live in the past, but you strengthen your friendships when you take time to "remember when. . . . "

Finally, thank God for your evergreen friends. They are among the most valuable gifts you'll be given in your lifetime.

Cherish them—and make sure they know they're cherished.

Enjoy them—and enjoy your perennial friendship . . . together!

Something to ponder . . .

Here's one of my favorite memories of a time spent with a friend . . .

Growing Together

Anybody you meet can have something to teach you. Anyone you meet can help you grow.

But we've found that you tend to learn the most from the people you trust the most. And that's why you can learn so much from your friends.

You teach each other.

You grow together.

And the friends you have known the longest may be the ones who teach you the most.

Both of us, for example, cherish certain special friends from our childhood precisely because we learned so much from them. These were the ones who taught us what life was like outside the often-painful worlds of our homes. They showed us possibilities, they encouraged us, and they helped us grow. We hope we did the same for them.

For Emilie, a girl named Allene was this kind of friend. They played cello together in the school orchestra, and Emilie learned from Allene that it is possible to compete without harboring envy or bad feelings. Allene was by far the better player—and almost always first chair—but she always treated Emilie as an equal, sharing the joy of music instead of lording it over her.

She also welcomed Emilie into her large, close-knit family, teaching her what it was like to live in an intact family unit. For Emilie, living in a fatherless home, that was a little glimpse of heaven. In turn, Emilie taught Allene some of the things she had learned about keeping house. Later, Allene was maid of honor at Emilie's wedding, and they're still in touch today by letter and an occasional telephone call. They even made it a point to attend and sit together with their husbands at their fortieth high school reunion.

Donna has a special group of school chums who were close friends from about second grade on and who still manage to get together once or twice a year. (They all showed up from all over the country to celebrate Donna's fiftieth birthday.) These girls, too, encouraged Donna and helped her grow—in loving if not always gentle ways. When Donna's mother wouldn't let her shave her legs or pluck her eyebrows, these friends actually held her down and did it for her! More seriously, they let her know that the mistreatment she occasionally suffered from her mother was not normal or acceptable.

Donna will never forget coming to school with a black eye. She thought that was the way things were, but her friend Susan threatened to call the police. That was a lesson of love that Donna never forgot.

As we grew older, we continued to learn from the friends we met, especially those who hung around to become friends of the heart.

From older, more experienced friends and relatives, we learned vital lessons in what it means to be a woman, a wife, a mother, a speaker, a writer. We went to school at the feet of women who had been there before us, and they led us into fruitful adulthood—and more fruitful friendships.

With our peers, at the same time, we learned by doing. We swapped ideas and tips. We learned from our mistakes and theirs. We shared magazine articles and helpful books, and we talked about what worked and what didn't.

Now that we're a little older, we're enjoying the privilege of learning from those who are younger than us. From our children, when they were children, we learned lessons of patience and a love deeper than anything we could imagine. Now we are learning from these young adults lessons in passion and commitment and forgiveness. And from other young friends and colleagues we are learning both what it means to pass along what we've learned and to be humble enough to gain wisdom from those who come behind us.

And what have we learned from each other?

There have been so many lessons: lessons in patience, lessons in assertiveness, lessons in generosity, how-to lessons for work and home. Emilie taught Donna how to raise chickens (we even built Donna's coop together!). Donna taught Emilie how to cook real Italian spaghetti "gravy" and to enjoy an occasional splurge on nutrition and calories.

But what we've been learning, most of all, is how to keep on being friends together.

How to enjoy each other.

How to care for each other.

And how to learn together and keep on learning.

And that may be the most important lesson of all.

The Joys of Mature Friendship

Mature is an unpleasant word for some people—sort of a euphemism for *old*. But think of what the word really means: ripe, seasoned, beautiful.

We think that a mature, long-term friendship—like a mature marriage—is one of life's supreme accomplishments, as well as one of life's most astonishing gifts. In our own long-term friendship we are just beginning to truly savor the special qualities this maturity has brought to our relationship.

And we have come to see maturity as a worthy goal for any friendship—something to shoot for, something to count on.

The thing is, as your friendships grow, you get better at being a friend . . . or at least you should. You've learned to winnow out the judgers, the fair-weather friends, the friends who are not really friends.

You've learned how to touch, how to give, how to keep your mouth shut when it's appropriate and speak when you need to speak.

Some things have grown less important to you—like status, like exclusivity, like always being right, like proving what a good friend you are.

Some things have grown more important—like acceptance, like keeping promises, like being trustworthy, like being careful when you hold your friend's heart, like spending time together, like the security of knowing you are loved.

We may or may not be better people at our age than we were at 20.

But we're certainly better friends.

And we think that's a wonderful thing to be.

Something to ponder . . .

*This is how my friend helps
me to grow . . .*

A Friendship Story

"Ours is a friendship that has lasted almost 50 years. We met in the eighth grade in Burkburnett, Texas. My father was a minister in a small Nazarene church there. I invited Maxine to come to church with me one Sunday, and that one event started a friendship that has continued to this day. We both married men from Sheppard Air Force Base, located not far from the church. Our husbands, Merl and Ed, roomed together on the base and were also best friends. Maxine and I stood up for each other's wedding during our senior year of high school. Over the next few years we each had three children. All of them in consecutive order were born months and, in one instance, only three days apart. Though this was unplanned, it seemed ironic that we were still doing things together.

"Through the years our lives were separated by the miles that took my minister husband and me far away to Pennsylvania. Even then, Max and I kept in touch by letters and phone calls whenever possible. Now, we are down to our retirement years in East Texas. Maxine and Ed moved within a mile and a half from us so that we could retire close to each other. What better ending than to repeat the beginning of our lives together?

"Time has changed many things, but one thing that has grown dearer with the years has been our friendship. Even today, many people ask if we are sisters. Those silly schoolgirl years have matured into an enduring, unconditional friendship between the two of us. Maxine has always been the ideal friend who holds in her heart the intimate secrets of my life, as I do hers. What more could I ask than for someone to know me better than I know myself and still love me? I wouldn't trade the laughter and the tears for one moment without my 'best friend.' There is no measure of wealth, no scale of greatness, no degree of success that could in any way replace a lifetime of friendship and blessing. God has given us this special gift of each other."

—Mary Klink,
Henderson, Texas

Ceremonies of Friendship

Here's a beautiful way to water and fertilize an evergreen friendship—to keep it green and flourishing year after year: Begin a tradition together, and make it a priority to keep that tradition going.

You probably already share a tradition or two, anyway. Rituals and traditions are part of any long-term relationship. A shared history is built in part on a foundation of "we always do this" together. But the specifics of what you do together will vary as widely as the personalities of your friends.

A friendship tradition can be something as simple as sharing a cup of tea while you chat on the phone or meeting for coffee on Saturday morning. It can be as elaborate as a planned annual reunion in the place you met, a party you throw together every year, or a big family barbecue on the Fourth of July.

It can be silly (sending the same funny card back and forth over the years).

It can be serious (meeting together to ask a blessing on any new home either of you moves into) or solemn (an annual candlelight dinner in which you affirm your friendship and vow to be friends for another year).

Some people have their pictures taken together every year.

Some people get together for the Oscars or the Superbowl.

Some people have been taking their families to the same summer house for decades on end.

Our own friendship thrives on a number of traditions—things we've been doing together for years and years. One is our December spa retreat, where we relax together in those wonderful terry robes and let the tensions of the year and the stresses of the season melt away.

Another is the smaller tradition of sharing tea and coffee together. Sometimes we enjoy Emilie's favorite: tea, sipped from Emilie's collection of porcelain teacups or from Middle Eastern chai glasses—a tradition in Donna's family. Sometimes we share Donna's favorite: good coffee, sipped from beautiful porcelain or earthenware mugs.

Still another old tradition we've enjoyed over the years is cooking together. We like to go out to eat, but we also love to share a kitchen, working in harmony to produce a simple but delicious meal. How we love to gather with our families around a table in Arizona or California, hold hands, and ask God's blessings on both our food and our friendship.

Those are just a few of the things we've always enjoyed doing together.

But we've started some new traditions as well—like our friendship ball.

What is a friendship ball? It's simply a round Christmas ornament that opens up to hold a tiny, inexpensive treasure: a single chocolate, a miniature book, a pile of coated paper clips, even a loving note. (Donna once sent a cassette, but that was cheating—it didn't really fit in the ball!) We send our friendship ball back and forth to each other all year, and we've come to count on discovering what it holds for us each time. We also find that we're always on the lookout for wonderful little "ball stuffers"!

Our friendship ball is a tradition we've kept up for about three years. The tradition has even expanded to include refurbishing the box the ball travels in. We plan to continue sending it back and forth as long as we possibly can—and we highly recommend this tradition as a fun way to keep a friendship fresh!

But you don't have to use an ornament, of course! It's the continuity of the thing, the reciprocity of the gesture, that makes the tradition such fun. Donna once carried out a similar tradition with a little coffee crock. We know friends who have shared a decorated box.

The joy, you see, is not really in the thing itself, though you will almost certainly have a good time.

The real joy is in the continuity, the faithfulness, the braiding together of our histories. The joy is in the ceremony, in the "we always do it."

And the real joy, of course, is having the evergreen friends to always do it with.

A Covenant between Friends

In a sense, the very existence of a long-term friendship is an unspoken promise. Every hour or day you spend together, every moment you invest in keeping in touch, is a tacit promise to spend another.

But have you ever thought of spelling out your promises in a shared covenant of friendship?

It's not for everyone, but it can be a special and strengthening experience.

A covenant is a pact between friends, a solemn promise, like a marriage vow. When you covenant with someone to be her friend, you're consciously signing up for the long haul. This is a friendship of the will, a chosen commitment to be together long term . . . for friendship's sake.

Donna has just that kind of connection with the six women in her *chaber* group. *Chaber* is a Hebrew word meaning "bound together." And that's exactly what they are— women with similar values who have made the choice to be bound together with a promise of friendship.

A friendship covenant is a vow to affirm one another, to be available to each other, to pray for one another, to share openly and risk honesty, to listen sensitively, to keep confidences, and to hold one another accountable.

It is also a promise to work out whatever problems arise for leaving the friendship is not an option.

That group has been going now for 15 years. And to be honest, those years have not always been smooth. Some people in the group have wanted out, although the whole point of the group is that there is no getting out. Some members have been disappointed. And the women in the group have not all turned out to be "best friends"; in fact, some if not all of the group members have other friends to whom they feel closer.

And yet, despite it all, there is a comfort in the knowledge that these people have pledged to be there for one another. Together they have already helped each other through a procession of difficulties: the loss of a child, marital difficulties, physical ailments. And they are counting on each other to still be there in the years to come. They're there for the long haul. And that's no small blessing.

Entering into a friendship covenant is not something to be taken lightly. It's not something you would consider with just any friend. Remember, it's for life! And it's not a legally binding contract, but a covenant—a solemn promise of the heart.

If after long thought and much prayer you believe a friendship covenant is for you and your friend, here's how you can go about it:

Take the time to write down what you are promising to do. Write down what you expect from each other. Make copies for each of you, and sign them in a solemn ceremony.

Light a candle.

Touch hands.

Then sign your names to promise that no matter what happens, no matter when, you choose to be bound together as friends.

Friends for the long haul.

As long as you both shall live . . . and maybe longer.

Long Distance

Distance doesn't always make the heart grow fonder.

And yet physical distance—even a very long distance—doesn't have to harm a friendship.

We know, because our own close friendship has been a long-distance one from the start. It has grown and thrived over the phone lines and the airlines and through the highway system and the mail system.

And ours is far from the only successful long-distance friendship we know. Some long-distance friends—pen pals and e-mail partners and telephone voices—have never even met in person! And plenty of other people have successfully kept a friendship humming long after one or both have had to pack their bags and move away.

As we and many others have discovered, a long-distance friendship even offers some distinct advantages over more "local" friendships.

In the first place, it's sometimes hard to know whether a person's your friend because of true affection or simply because of proximity and convenience. With a long-distance friend you know the answer. You know that a friend who takes the trouble to nurture a long-distance friendship is truly a friend who loves you. If she didn't, why would she take the trouble?

In the second place, long-distance friendships are actually less vulnerable to disruptions than local ones. What does it matter, for instance, if one of you moves or your circumstances change? You may not be sure you'll stay in touch with your local friends, but you know that nothing has changed with your long-distance ones. They'll still be available, just as they always have! A friend of ours who recently made two family moves to two different states in two years tells us that the long-distance friendships she maintained before the moves have continued to be her lifeline while she struggles to make new local friendships and to convert her former local friendships into long-distance ones.

Best of all, precisely because she doesn't see and interact with you every day, a long-distance friend can provide a valuable perspective your local friends might not be able to manage. She can see things more clearly because she's less involved with the ins and outs of your daily life. She can show you the forest while you're still busy stumbling through the trees. She can be a touchstone to remind you of who you are and what you're supposed to be about, even when you've lost sight of your purposes and goals. Having access to that kind of perspective is truly a wonderful gift.

Despite the distinct advantages of a long-distance friendship, however, the drawbacks are clear as well.

Chief among them is that a long-distance friendship is by definition . . . well, distant. Getting together involves more planning and expense. Communicating costs more, too—even a simple "snail mail" letter requires a third of a dollar—and sometimes seems to take forever. (Have you ever written a long letter to a distant friend, mailed it, and then just had to call her up to talk?) With cross-country or international friendships, time differences can make communication even more tricky.

Cultivating and nourishing a long-distance relationship usually requires more intentionality as well on the part of both friends. You have to keep each other in mind because you're not likely to be reminded by a chance encounter or a stray remark. You both have to care enough to give your relationship priority. And you both have to be willing to forgive the inevitable lapses when one friend gets busy and seems to drop off the face of the earth. Such things can happen even in local friendships, but they happen more readily when there is a cushion of distance between you.

Most difficult of all is the inability to touch a long-distance friend or look into her face. You miss out on her daily companionship. You can't call her up at the last minute and catch a movie or go shopping. You can't solicit a hug on a difficult day or the touch of a hand when you're under the weather. Inevitably, you miss out on sharing everyday moments.

It's because of this inherent distance, this lack of immediacy, that some long-distance friendships do drift apart. Nobody plans it, but the demands of everyday life seem to push the long-distance letter or the necessary phone call into the background. That's when guilt sets in, and a vicious pattern begins that, if not arrested, can spell the slow death of a treasured friendship.

We've heard the story from many people: First, you get busy or distracted and let communication slide between you. You forget to write. You don't call. Her birthday slips by unnoticed.

Next, you feel guilty. You feel bad about the emotional distance between you, and you would like to make up for it. But you feel that now you need to make some sort of a big gesture—a specially chosen gift, an eloquent letter—to make up for your neglect. (This is probably your pride talking.) But because you're still busy and distracted, you just can't manage that beautiful gesture you would like to make.

What comes next? More guilt! Now when you think of the relationship, you feel bad. So consciously or unconsciously, you put off thinking about it.

Finally, silence is easier, but it's a sad silence. Eventually one of you may move, and you'll lose track of each other completely. Or you'll hold on to each other's addresses but avoid each other out of embarrassment or those old feelings of guilt.

That's a pitiful thing—to let a valuable friendship drift because of neglect and guilt. But it happens all the time. We've talked to so many people who speak with regret of the friendships they've let get away.

The good news is that there is a cure for friendship drift. There's even a solution for snaring a friendship that's already started to float away. It's very simple: Simply break the cycle!

First, you need to swallow your pride and set your guilt aside.

Then you need to make contact. Pick up the phone. Write an e-mail. Scribble a note on a postcard.

Say, "Hello. I've missed you."

Say, "Hi, how are things?"

Best of all, say, "I still love you! When can we get together again?"

15 Great Ideas for Staying Close When You're Far Away

1. *Organize a reunion.* How often you do this will depend on time, distance, finances, and many other factors. But if at all possible, try to get together in person at least once a year. One of you can visit the other, or you can meet at a central location.

2. *Invest in Ma Bell.* The telephone can be a lifeline between long-distance friends. Think of the bills as investments in your friendship. (If you're on a tight budget, a separate phone card for friend calls can help you stick to your budget.)

3. *Don't forget to write.* There's just something special about receiving a card or letter in the mailbox. A letter, unlike a phone call, can be reread and treasured for years.

4. *Go high tech.* If you have a computer or fax, explore the advantages of using these high-tech tools to keep in touch. E-mail is an especially handy, immediate, and inexpensive way to keep current with long-distance friends. Some of our friends tells us it's revitalized their faraway friendships.

5. *Send pictures.* This is a great way to keep current with each other's lives. Do you have duplicate shots of the same pose? Send one to your friend with a note on the back. Why not keep a special album in your home to stash your friend's pictures as they come?

6. *Vacation together.* Meet somewhere between your homes for a week of fun and renewing your friendship. Check out hotels, resorts, spas, or retreat centers.

7. *Work together on a long-distance project.* Planning a college reunion or cosponsoring a child from another country give you an excuse and a reminder to stay in close touch.

8. *At least say hi.* During very busy times when you barely have time to breathe, much less write or even phone, a simple postcard or a five-minute phone call can still keep the lines of communication open.

9. *Maintain a tradition like a friendship ball.* See page 122 for details.

10. *Treasure twin mementos.* Emilie found twin teacups in an antique store and gave one to her friend Anne. Now whenever either of them sips from that cup, she thinks of the other person.

11. *Pray for each other*—always and faithfully.

12. *Exchange videotapes of your homes and families.* Be creative. Write a script and make it like a "real" film. Have your family help you with the production. Even get your animals involved.

13. *Exchange audiocassettes sharing your love for each other.*

14. *Send your friend a subscription or enroll her in an "of the month" club.* Whether it's magazines, books, flowers, fruits, or even steaks, the monthly arrival will bring thoughts of you. Just be sure the subscription doesn't require your friend to do something or pay something! (The "negative option" clubs aren't the best kind of gift!)

15. *Send her a favorite recipe with a batch of results.* Send it next-day mail so it arrives fresh. A variation of this idea would be to send a regional specialty by overnight mail. One friend we know even sent her friend a whole salmon packed in dry ice!

A Friendship Story

"Forty-seven years ago my Great Aunt Bell (a retired teacher) said to an eight-year-old girl in Liverpool, England, 'You will write to my niece.' It wasn't a suggestion or a request, but a simple directive. So Brenda Hartley picked up her fountain pen and wrote her first letter to me in Los Angeles, California.

"I could not believe the envelope, let alone the letter, had been written by a child my same age. The handwriting was so delicate and precise, it could have been printed by a machine. But I was delighted to have received this mysterious "foreign" mail from the other side of the world, and in my *much* less elegant eight-year-old American handwriting, I answered her letter.

"Thus began a correspondence that led to a deep friendship that has endured for these 47 years and counting. We watched with joy and amazement how our lives have paralleled over the years. We struggled through childhood, adolescence, universities, boyfriends, weddings, childbirths, and deaths. We both became elementary school teachers, married, and had daughters—three for Bren and two for me.

"We did not meet until we were 24 years old. I had been married for two years and had a baby daughter when Brenda first came to America. She returned home, got engaged, married, and we didn't see each other again for 20 years. The letters continued consistently, although there were occasional gaps when one or the other or both of us were preoccupied with young families.

"My oldest daughter, Amy, was able to visit Bren and Pete and girls while attending a summer session at Cambridge University in England. She came home and said, 'Mom, you have to go to England before you are too old! They are *just* like us!' The next summer Amy and I went, and I saw what she meant. We were *so* much more alike than different, even though we had been raised oceans apart. . . .

"It seems we have shared all of life's joys and sorrows, surprises and blessings, even though we are a continent apart. Although my Aunt Bell ('Auntie') is in heaven now, I hope she knows how much that one little comment, 'You will write to my niece,' changed my life."

—Carolyn C. Alex,
Santa Ana, California

Thinking about Good-bye

These days, though we don't talk about it much, we are thinking about having to say good-bye.

Perhaps not for a while. (We hope.) But perhaps soon.

Not because we have any inclination to be apart, but because of the cancer that has taken its inconvenient and unwelcome place in the middle of Emilie's life these days.

Nobody's given up yet, and so far the news is promising.

But still, there's nothing like a serious illness to focus the mind on what's really important.

Like the beauty of God's creation.

Like the preciousness of our families.

Like the inexpressible blessing we have in our friends.

And how hard it's going to be to say good-bye, whenever the day might come.

We pray it might be later rather than sooner.

But we're trying to keep our focus the same, regardless of how many days and hours are left us to be friends here on earth.

We want to hold each other close.

We want to create warm memories, not regrets.

We want to embrace every moment that we're together—every giggle, every teardrop, every hug, every heartache.

We want to say the things that need saying, but guard our tongue from the hurtful and the unnecessary.

We want to affirm the life, the hope, the joy that has lived in our friendship year after year.

We want to live fully in that life and hope and joy, so that our good-bye—whenever it may be—will be a sweet farewell . . . with a promise of eternity.

For something in us tells us we'll always be friends—the dearest friends of the heart.

18 Ways to Tell Your Friend You Love Her

1. Give her a hug.
2. Write her a poem.
3. Plant a tree in her honor.
4. Clean her house, do her laundry, or cook dinner for her family.
5. Take her out to breakfast.
6. Help her practice for a test or an interview.
7. Embrace the people she loves.
8. Kidnap her for a Girls' Night Out.
9. Encourage her to take care of herself.
10. Give her something that is meaningful to you.
11. Throw her a surprise party.
12. Send her flowers.
13. Make her a pillow or a pie or a poem.
14. Rub her feet.
15. Give her a picture of the two of you in a beautiful frame.
16. Buy her a warm hat or a pair of fuzzy slippers.
17. Take over an obligation or responsibility so she can do something she really wants to do.
18. Just say it: "Your friendship is a treasure to me."

Epilogue

Through the Ages

To my friend . . .

When we're small, our friends are our playmates. We ride bikes and chase butterflies and giggle and pretend. We share our toys and our secrets.

You're my friend. You're always fun to play with.

As we grow, our friends are our lifelines. When parents fight or siblings tease or algebra has us stumped . . . we know we have an ally. Friends offer a friendly face when life doesn't seem friendly. They're a voice on the phone that reminds us we're not alone. We share our problems and our hiding places and our unwavering loyalty.

You're my friend. With you I always feel safe.

As we learn to be women, our friends are our mirrors. We pore through magazines and compare notes and tell what our mothers said and gradually figure out what it means to be who we are. We learn to shave our legs and we ponder the meaning of life. We share our wardrobes and our dreams.

You're my friend. You remind me of who I am and who I can be.

As we launch into life's responsibilities, our friends are our helpers. We type for each other and cook for each other and pitch in with carpools and committees. We run errands and do favors. We share the load.

You're my friend. Thanks for everything you do!

As we maneuver among life's milestones, our friends are our support. We show up for concerts and recitals and weddings and funerals. We dispense tea and coffee and lots of sympathy. We listen and listen and listen and sometimes give advice. But everything we say is really another form of "I believe in you." We share our strength.

You're my friend. I couldn't make it without you.

As we move on in life, our friends are our companions— sometimes our only companions. We eat together. We go to the gym or walk the mall. We work puzzles and dig in the garden and hike mountain trails in each other's company. Usually we talk and talk . . . but sometimes we're just silent together. We share our lives.

You're my friend. I cherish the hours I spend with you.

You're my friend, and still
my beloved companion . . .

You're my stalwart supporter . . .
my indispensable helper . . .
my mirror of insight . . .
my lifeline of hope and encouragement.

You're my friend.
I love you!

(Can you come out and play?)

_❧ ❧ ❧_

A final word for all
our friends . . .

"I thank my God upon
every remembrance of you."

—THE BOOK OF PHILIPPIANS

_❧ ❧ ❧_

*T*o obtain information about
Emilie Barnes' seminars, tapes,
and other helpful time-management
products, send a self-addressed,
stamped envelope to:

More Hours in My Day
2838 Rumsey Drive
Riverside, California 92506

AND

If you have any questions or comments, or if
you would like to have Donna address your
group, contact her at:

Mrs. David Otto
11453 N. 53rd Place
Scottsdale, AZ 85254